Potty Training in (5) Easy Steps

Potty Training
in 5 Easy Steps

A SIMPLE GUIDE FOR PARENTS

Allison Jandu

**ROCKRIDGE
PRESS**

For general information on our other products and services or to obtain technical support, please contact our Customer Care Department within the U.S. at (866) 744-2665, or outside the U.S. at (510) 253-0500.

Rockridge Press publishes its books in a variety of electronic and print formats. Some content that appears in print may not be available in electronic books, and vice versa.

TRADEMARKS: Rockridge Press and the Rockridge Press logo are trademarks or registered trademarks of Callisto Media Inc. and/or its affiliates, in the United States and other countries, and may not be used without written permission. All other trademarks are the property of their respective owners. Rockridge Press is not associated with any product or vendor mentioned in this book.

Interior and Cover Designer: Angie Chiu
Art Producer: Sue Bischofberger
Editor: Brian Sweeting
Production Editor: Andrew Yackira
Production Manager: Martin Worthington

Cover illustration © 2021 Drew Bardana
All interior illustrations used under license from The Noun Project
Author photo courtesy of © Dunks Photo

ISBN: Print 978-1-64876-741-8
eBook 978-1-64876-742-5
R0

FOR EVAN AND LAYLA:
Without you I never would
have realized my true passion—
being your mom.

CONTENTS

INTRODUCTION

HI! MY NAME IS ALLISON. Thank you for choosing me to go on this exciting adventure with you! If you're like most people, you're probably a little nervous about ditching the diapers, which is normal. I just happen to possess a love and enthusiasm for potty training. Maybe that makes me a bit of a weirdo, but I'm okay with that!

I'm a professional potty training consultant, author, wife, and mom of two awesome little people. I've helped hundreds of families with kids from ages 14 months to 11 years old, of all personalities and abilities, and I'm proud to boast a 98% success rate. I work hands-on with children, parents, and daycare providers, so I know the potty training process inside and out from multiple perspectives.

I've got to be honest though—I never thought that I'd be teaching kids how to pee and poop in the potty for a living. But my career stemmed from my experiences potty training my own two kids, and you may be surprised to learn that it wasn't all cupcakes and rainbows! My son, who is my oldest, first helped me realize my love for potty training. Since I was a working mom myself, it was a great opportunity to spend time together, and seeing how proud he was as he refined his new skill was intoxicating. I couldn't understand why so many people dreaded potty training.

It wasn't until I started to potty train my daughter years later that I really got a taste of how difficult the process can be. I knew she was ready, but she was resisting all my efforts. I reassessed, made some adjustments, and figured out how to adapt to her unique way of learning. I was able to get her diaper free at 20 months within just a couple of days. All my friends and family were so intrigued. I started helping them potty train their kids, all with the same success, and, hence, the idea of the "potty training consultant" was born.

I've written this book as a practical solution to potty training for you—the busy parent who's trying to balance multiple responsibilities. As a busy mom myself, I get that it's not realistic to find three or more days in a row to focus on potty training. I want to take away some of that pressure and guide you through the best way to potty train on your own timeline. I cover techniques that will be effective no matter your child's age and personality or the amount of time you have to dedicate to the process.

But this is not your typical how-to potty program. Instead, I lay out the steps in such a way that you can take as much or as little time as you need to accomplish each one. The phases could end up overlapping, so you may need to move on and read step 3 even before you've fully mastered everything in step 2. I'm not promising you an overnight solution. The entire process could end up taking you a few weeks or more, but that's perfectly okay. Potty training doesn't need to be condensed into one solid chunk of time in order for you and your child to see results.

Here's what you'll learn:

- How **you** can prepare for potty training. If you have a plan in place as your child's teacher and coach, you're bound to succeed.

- The best times to start potty training, how to determine when your child is ready and capable, and how to get them on board with the process. I'll also cover how to handle different personality types, because there is no one-size-fits-all potty training method!

- A proven, effective process for getting your child out of their diapers and onto the potty. I'll cover how to handle successes and accidents.

- How to transfer from potty training at home to your child's caregiver or daycare, so you can keep the momentum going even when your child isn't with you.

- How to get your child from "in training" to "fully trained"—my best practices for tackling naptime, nighttime, and poop training.

My goal with this book is to give you a big boost of confidence as you approach this new parenting experience. I want you come out of potty training sharing my same enthusiasm—or at least saying, "That wasn't so bad!" Potty training is a huge milestone in your child's life, and it's something that should be celebrated, not dreaded. Once you see how proud your child is as they master this new lifelong skill, you won't regret any of it, I promise. Let's dive in!

STEP 1
Set Yourself Up for Success

ONE OF THE MOST CHALLENGING PARTS OF potty training can be determining when and where to start. It can seem as though, in your busy world, there really is no perfect time to potty train. I always say potty training should be a marathon, not a sprint. And you can't go out and run a marathon to the finish line without training for it first. So if you do some preparation, like you are by reading this book, you're already setting yourself up for success. Here are the things that will give you the confidence you need to do it and do it right.

MYTHS AND MISCONCEPTIONS

With all of the information available on potty training, it's very difficult to determine what has true merit. Before I start telling you what to do, I'm going to start off by covering some of the most common misconceptions floating around out there that are just plain wrong—and are likely holding you back from achieving potty training success.

"Potty training is one of the hardest parts of parenting."

Actually, potty training can be a great opportunity to create a bonding experience with your child. In the busyness of day-to-day life, it's easy to get caught up in making sure chores are done and everyone is in bed on time, and in the process forget to really appreciate the little things and the small moments you spend with your child (I'm speaking from personal experience here). Potty training essentially *forces* us to spend time together—but instead of just sitting around waiting for the next accident, take the opportunity to create some extra special time doing things you both enjoy that you wouldn't otherwise get a chance to do. The potty training will be happening, but it doesn't need to be unpleasant, tedious, and all-consuming.

The moral of the story? Line up some fun activities to do with your child while potty training. When you put in the effort to make your child happy, the experience will be more enjoyable for you, and your child will be more likely to try and make you happy by using the potty correctly. It's a win-win!

"There is only one right way to potty train."

The truth is, there is absolutely no one-size-fits-all potty training method. What works for one child most likely will not work for the next. Every child has their own unique personality and potty learning style. But personality isn't the only factor that should determine how you potty train. It's also extremely important to consider your family's lifestyle, so you can choose a process that will fit as seamlessly as possible into your daily routine.

> **The moral of the story?** Don't compare your situation with anyone else's. Your child is unique, and your potty training journey will be, too.

"Girls are easier to potty train than boys."

No one can speak more strongly to the inaccuracy of this statement than I can. My son was a total breeze to potty train, and my daughter was the epitome of a potty training nightmare. I work with an equal number of parents of girls and boys who struggle with potty training. Most of the time, difficult potty training situations boil down to a personality trait—of the parent or the child—that's clashing with the approach.

> **The moral of the story?** Gender does not matter when it comes to potty training. Be prepared based on your child's personality and way of learning—and yours—and you will succeed.

"Disposable training pants are an essential tool for potty training."

Disposable trainers were created to be used as a transition between diapers and underwear. They provide the same absorbency as a diaper to contain any mess but offer the feel of underwear because they can be pulled up and down. But they're not necessary when it comes to potty training. In fact, they can even prolong the process because they are just too similar to diapers for your child to know and feel the difference. It's important that your child understands there is no longer going to be something there to catch their mess when they pee or poop.

> **The moral of the story?** Save your money or invest in some cloth training pants instead. Disposable trainers may be convenient, but they're only going to hinder your child's potty progress. (Later in the book I'll note some exceptions to this.)

"It should be your child's choice to start potty training."

The notion of waiting for your child to be ready was made popular by famous pediatrician Dr. T. Berry Brazelton. He suggested the child should make the choice to initiate potty training as opposed to the parents introducing the idea. Dr. Brazelton also believed that training too early could have negative effects later on. However, there is no scientific evidence to prove that theory. The average potty training age in the United States steadily increased from just 18 months in the 1950s to 37 months by 2001, likely due to the combination of the affordability and convenience of disposable diapers and the growing popularity of this new philosophy.

Not only is this statement not scientifically proven, there's also no guarantee that your child will *ever* initiate using the potty on their own, which can leave you backed into a corner. Many parents end up not being able to send their children to school because they're still in diapers. In most cases, schools have diaper-changing resources only for children with disabilities.

> **The moral of the story?** Start potty training when YOU are ready. If you're prepared in your role as your child's teacher with the best methods available, then potty training will be a successful and rewarding experience for you both.

WHEN TO BEGIN

I want to start by saying there are no hard-and-fast rules as to when you should start potty training—no matter what your opinionated grandmother might say! The main things to consider are where your child is in their development, how willing you are to commit, and how potty training will fit into your current lifestyle.

Development Is Key

Even though there are several factors to consider before starting potty training, your child's development is the most important. Studies have shown that the average child is physiologically ready to potty train around the age of 18 months. That basically means their brains can handle the concept, and their bodies can execute it. Does this indicate that we all should be potty training as soon as our children turn 18 months old? Of course not! In addition to the biological nature of potty training, your child should also possess basic communication skills (either verbal or physical), have a good handle on gross motor skills such as walking and sitting, and be able to understand and apply basic direction. Typically these traits all present themselves around the age of 22 to 28 months, making this the ideal age to introduce potty training from a developmental perspective.

I know some of you might be thinking, *Oh no! I already missed that window.* It's okay! You definitely aren't alone. And the window is not closed. Just because you might be starting the process later doesn't in any way mean you've failed. Above all, it's most important to make sure you're prepared and in a confident place as your child's teacher and coach before you dive in. In the following steps, I'll be walking you through how to best prepare.

Starting Earlier (22 to 28 months)

There are pros and cons to introducing potty training at a younger age. I'll cover the pros first. Younger children are typically able to adapt to change easily, they're eager to please and seek approval from you, they tend to want to mimic things they see adults doing, they haven't necessarily found or exerted their individuality just yet, and it's easy for you to reward them with simple verbal praise. You can also take into account that you're instilling a sense of empowerment and independence in your child by teaching them to use the potty, which improves their self-confidence overall. And let's not forget to mention all the money you'll save on diapers by potty training earlier!

But there can also be certain challenges associated with training a younger child. Examples of these would be having to provide assistance getting your child to the potty or toilet, helping them use it, and participating in undressing and dressing. Younger children also typically urinate more frequently and have less advanced muscle control than do children just a few months older.

If you train significantly earlier (before your child is 18 months old), your daycare or preschool has likely not introduced potty training yet, so whatever potty training you work on at home may not be carried over into the playroom or classroom just yet. We'll discuss this more in step 4.

Starting Later (30 months and up)

As you may have guessed, there are also pros and cons to waiting until later to potty train. Some benefits to potty training older children include less assistance required when using the potty and undressing/dressing, more advanced muscle control (usually), and better understanding of the concept of the promise of a reward.

There are also challenges you're likely to run into when potty training a child on the older end of the spectrum. The main issue is a stronger resistance to change. As kids get older, they get more comfortable in their everyday routines, diapers included. If you think about it, our children have diapers on from minutes after birth, and that's all they've known their entire lives. It's understandable if they show some resistance when you ask them to use this newfangled contraption of a potty instead! Add to that, they now need to stop playing and relocate to the potty whenever nature calls. By now your child has probably started to find (or has already found) their voice as an individual little person, and if there's something they don't want to do, they're sure to let you know about it!

If you wait significantly later (three-and-a-half years and up), you're also likely to be met with societal limits such as requirements your child be potty trained in order to go to school, camps, or athletics programs. Although potty training under a deadline is still doable, it tends to raise everyone's stress levels, which can end up making things a little more challenging.

Now that I've presented you with the facts, you can use them to weigh your options and choose what you think works best for you and your child. Once you've decided, don't let anyone convince you otherwise.

SIGNS YOUR CHILD IS READY

Now that we've established the best *time* to start potty training, let's talk about some signs you can look for to determine if your child is developmentally ready, aside from what I already mentioned in the previous section. It's good to keep in mind that your child doesn't need to demonstrate all of these markers before you get started. There are some kids who never exhibit any obvious signs, and that's okay, too! Use your parental instincts to assess their potential.

Staying Dry for Two Hours or More

A child's natural progression of bowel/bladder control goes something like this:

- First, they'll stop pooping in their sleep (hallelujah). This may have already happened, as many babies nix this by their first birthday.

- Next, your child will gain daytime bowel (poop) control. You may start to notice patterns and even be able to predict at what times they'll poop throughout the day.

- Around this same time they'll develop a certain level of daytime bladder (pee) control. This is when you'll notice them staying dry for longer periods during the day.

- Last comes nighttime bladder (pee) control, which is a result of improved muscle strength, a neurological connection between the brain and bladder, and hormonal development.

Once you notice your child needs less frequent diaper changes, it's a good time to start potty training, especially if they're staying dry for naps and/or overnight. If they aren't quite there yet, just feel their diaper during the day every hour or so to get an idea of how often they're peeing. Make a mental note. Does it seem to be continual small pees or one larger pee every so often? If it's the latter, you have the green light to introduce that potty!

Asking to Have Their Diaper Changed

This is another big sign because it means that your child is becoming aware of their body's functions and when they happen. It also means that they probably don't like the feeling of being wet or dirty, and this is a great incentive to use the potty instead of a diaper! If they have pooped, you can start explaining that poop likes to be in the potty. (Hey, we've probably said stranger things to our kids!) Take it a step further and empty the poop from the diaper into the toilet and say, "Bye-bye, poopy!" while they flush. This helps them make the connection that poop really belongs in the potty.

Hiding When Pooping

Children hide when they need to poop because they want privacy. You see, even at a young age, we develop this innate understanding that pooping is something private and personal. This is why some kids get embarrassed—not because it's inherently shameful, but because they're beginning to understand that it isn't socially acceptable to poop in front of others. This leaves them to poop only when they're left alone or when they have access to their favorite hiding place.

This is a good sign to start potty training for two reasons. First, it means that they know they need to poop *before* they actually start going (which means that theoretically they could stop what they're doing and go sit on the potty instead of going behind the couch). Second, it gives *you* a better indication of when they are pooping so you can start taking note of their routine. Then once you do ditch the diapers, you can be paying extra attention around these times to help them get success on the potty—even if it means you can't be in the room or you have to move the potty behind the couch for the time being. It can also allow you to be proactive and prevent constipation if you know they haven't gone when they normally would have.

Showing Interest in the Bathroom/Potty Training

Is your little one always following you into the bathroom? I know it can be annoying (can we just have one minute to pee in peace?!), but it's actually a good thing when it comes to potty training. Your child is just curious about where you're sneaking off to every so often and what goes on when you sit on that strange-looking chair with the water in it. Your child's natural curiosity provides the opportunity to make these times a fun learning experience! Walk them through step-by-step what you're doing, even have them help you by "reading" you a story or handing you some toilet paper. This takes away any apprehension surrounding that unknown realm of the bathroom, helps them become familiar with the general process, and could even encourage them to want to give it a try!

DIFFERENT PERSONALITY TRAITS

One of the most fun things about parenthood is watching your child develop their own little personality. We usually start to get a handle on their general temperament from very early on, but it isn't until the toddler years that their true character starts to show itself. It's important to recognize and speak to your child's unique personality and potty learning style when deciding how to potty train them. That being said, here are some of the best ways to handle the different challenges associated with the most classic personality types.

Strong-Willed/Opinionated

I think most parents would probably describe their toddlers this way! But don't worry, just because your child is strong-willed or stubborn doesn't mean they'll be difficult to potty train—as long as you know the best way to approach them before you get started. Strong-willed children are stubborn because they're creatures of habit and they love to feel in control. Typically, everything needs to be their idea, they are stuck in their ways, and tantrums/meltdowns are more prevalent. Sound familiar?

Since these kiddos don't do well with change, they're going to need to be eased into the idea of potty training. It can help to count down the days to "no more diapers" on the calendar. Choose three to five days before you get started and "X" off the day together each morning (unless you feel like this would cause them stress or anxiety). Either way, take the opportunity to build their confidence and empower them. Once the process starts, you have to allow them to have a certain level of control (or perceived control). They aren't going to respond well to being told when to use the potty or using the potty at set time intervals. Instead, follow their lead, use simple prompts, and don't be afraid to offer rewards. At the same time, they're likely going to be testing you to see if you'll give them back their diapers, so remember to stay firm. Don't feel guilty about enforcing the new rules, and try to react only to their *good* potty behavior.

Thinker/Introvert

This child tends to be an observer. You can just see the gears turning when they discover something new. They are usually shy, tend to be more comfortable around adults than around other children, and like to play independently.

If this describes your little one, you'll do well introducing them to potty training in the form of books or videos online. A doll that drinks and wets can be a great tool for these children because it will really help them understand the mechanics of the body. In this group, there will be kids on each end of the spectrum when it comes to privacy. Some won't release on the potty if you're in the room, and some are going to want you holding them while they sit. Be sure you're doing your best to make them feel comfortable. You could also encounter challenges at daycare or with another caregiver because the thinker/introvert child may be too shy to let someone know they need to use the potty. It helps to have a mini-conference with you, your child, and the caregiver so your child understands it's okay to ask for help.

Laid-Back/Easygoing

This is the kind of child who doesn't mind if you forgot to pack their favorite sippy cup on your family vacation. You know, the kind of kid who makes you want to have more children (*wink*). They're good at sharing and strive to seek your approval. They're able to go with the flow without much resistance and likely won't protest getting rid of diapers or sitting on the potty when prompted, making them fairly easy to potty train.

However, laid-back/easygoing children can be easily distracted or caught up in play, which can make them more prone to pee or poop accidents. They also may not be particularly bothered by the accidents when they happen. So don't be *too* casual. Still, make it clear that the new expectation is that pee/poop now go only in the potty. Using a timer can work well, so they have a predetermined time of when to stop playing and use the potty.

Extrovert/Silly

This child is always keeping you on your toes and is a ball of fun. They have no problem going up to a stranger and saying, "You look like Santa Claus!" They're usually very verbal and play well with others (although they're typically the leader of the pack). They might sometimes have a hard time sitting still or exhibiting appropriate behavior in certain environments. They also like to be the center of attention.

When you first introduce potty training to this child, look for books and videos that are fun and silly. Once you dive into potty training, keep a special basket of toys and books near the potty that they only get to play with or read during potty time. This child might find potty accidents funny and will try to get a reaction out of you in any way possible (with good or bad potty behavior), so do your best to only react to the *good* potty behavior and be minimal and matter-of-fact when there is an accident.

SCRIPT

You can use the following questions to help gauge your child's readiness for potty training. They're designed to give you room to shape them the way that makes sense for you and your child. Let your child's answers guide you.

"Do you want to help Mommy make your sandwich?"
An eagerness to help is a great characteristic to have before starting potty training.

"Can you put all the red blocks in this basket?"
See if your child is able to complete simple tasks without much direction.

"Oh, you need a new diaper? Did you go pee or poop?"
Engaging them with this question gets them to connect the cause and effect.

"Is your diaper wet or dry?"
After they answer, check yourself to see if they were right. If so, be sure to praise them for knowing the difference!

"How does your belly feel right now?"
Ask this question if you see your child sneaking off to poop.

MAJOR CHANGES TO CONSIDER

Before deciding to start potty training, try to think about any upcoming changes or events that could potentially cause your child (or you) any kind of emotional stress. Common examples would be:

- Divorce

- A recent or upcoming move

- A job change

- A new school or daycare

- The arrival of a new sibling

Obviously, a lot of these circumstances are unavoidable, but that's okay! Overall, you want to make sure that things have settled back into a regular routine before getting rid of diapers, not only for your child's sake, but for yours, as well. With emotional stress comes the possibility of regression, and you are busy enough as it is without having to potty train the same child twice!

In the case of divorce, it's super important that both parents be on the same page when it comes to potty training. If your child knows they'll get a diaper when they get to one parent's house, you can kiss goodbye any hopes of them using the potty at the other's. It can be helpful to have a written plan in place that is agreed upon and is realistic for both households.

Moving to a new school or daycare is not only stressful for your child, but there is also the potential that the rules and practices for potty training are now different from what they were before. Be sure to ask the teacher or director what their standard procedures are, so you can make any necessary adjustments at home, as well. Additionally, explore the new classroom and bathroom with your child to help them feel more comfortable.

There's probably nothing more disruptive for your child than welcoming a new baby into the family. Try to involve big brother or sister in the everyday care of the baby, especially the diaper-change process. Allow them to hand you a new diaper and throw the old one away in the diaper pail. This makes them feel included and helpful, and participating in baby care also solidifies for your child the fact that *babies* wear diapers. In seeing your interaction with the new baby, your child may start to connect diapers to getting attention from you. Instead, offer that attention in other ways, such as some one-on-one time after the baby goes to sleep at night.

No matter the change, always keep the lines of communication with your child open. Validate any concerns they have without making them worse, and help them find the positives in a situation. Choosing a nonstressful time in your family's life will help set the best stage for potty training.

TROUBLESHOOTING TECHNIQUES

What do I do if my child isn't exhibiting any signs of readiness?

First of all, don't worry. It doesn't mean something is wrong or that they're below average in any way. Some kids never do show any of the classic signs. When this is the case, you'll need to rely less on typical markers and more on your child's physiological capability and your preparedness to get the job done. Remember, most children are *capable* of potty training around the two-year mark, whether or not they show any signs. So it's still going to be easiest on you to not put it off for too long. Get yourself set up with a plan of action, stick with it, and have confidence that they (and you!) can do this. Changing diapers will be a distant memory soon enough.

What if my child is a combination of personality types?
This is super common, and some children may even seem to have different personalities around different people or in different situations. Is your little one the golden child at preschool but turns into the Tasmanian Devil as soon as you pick them up? Take that into consideration when starting to potty train! It means you may need to adjust your behaviors and practices a little. There's nothing wrong with mixing up my suggestions and preparation activities depending on what you think will work for your child. I may be the expert on potty training, but you are the expert on your child.

What if I'm ready to start potty training, but daycare is not on board?
Parents who want to potty train on the earlier end of the spectrum can sometimes encounter this problem. It definitely shouldn't hold you back from introducing the idea of the potty at home; however, don't ditch the diapers cold turkey just yet if your child is still required to wear them at daycare. It will just end up confusing them and hinder their progress, and you'll be putting in extra effort for longer than necessary (and nobody wants that!). Instead, request a meeting with the daycare director to find out when they expect your child to move to a classroom where potty training will be a focus. Then see if they're willing to move your child up sooner. Learn about their potty practices in detail so you can incorporate them into what you do at home, to maintain as much consistency as possible. I'll talk about this in detail in step 4.

STEP 1 RECAP: FIVE TAKEAWAYS

1. Ignore the many common myths and misconceptions that are out there about potty training. Surround yourself with a support system of people who will be by your side to listen, without pushing unwanted opinions and advice.

2. Weigh the pros and cons about training earlier (younger than 22 months) versus later (older than 30 months). Decide what's a better fit for you and your family. On the fence? Remember that from a developmental perspective, the ideal age to potty train is between 22 and 28 months.

3. Evaluate your child's developmental readiness for potty training. Remember to look for signs such as staying dry for longer periods, or for naps and overnight, asking to have their diaper changed, hiding to poop, a general interest in the bathroom, and ability to follow basic directions.

4. Assess your child's personality type so you can identify their learning style and the best ways to approach potty training for them as an individual.

5. Think about your schedule for the next few months and consider any major changes or events. Make a point to write potty training on the calendar after everything has settled back into a normal routine.

STEP 2
Set Your Child Up for Success

NOW THAT YOU'VE TAKEN CARE OF the first, and possibly the most important step—preparing yourself—it's time to introduce the concept of potty training to your little one. Remember that children are creatures of habit, so it may not come easy to them to ditch the diapers. Your child's been doing just fine until now, so why would they want to change? But there are lots of ways to get them excited and to make potty training fun. The key is going to be building their confidence and empowering them into believing they can do it.

INTRODUCE THE POTTY

Introducing the concept of potty training to your child may seem daunting, but it doesn't need to be! There are a lot of ways to ease them into using the potty without stress, such as showing them the potty early and taking them to the bathroom with you when you go.

Introducing the Toilet

The earlier you're able to introduce the potty to your child, the better. Even if your child is very young, get a small potty chair and keep it in their room or next to the big potty in the bathroom so they can see it on a regular basis. In this case, the simpler the look of the potty the better because you don't want to promote it as a toy. Instead, keep it for just "business" and sit them on it between diaper changes every so often—they may surprise you and actually go! This is a great no-pressure approach to help your child get familiar with the concept, so it doesn't seem like as much of a big, scary change when the time comes to potty train.

If your child is already a little older and they don't have any potty experience yet, that's okay, too! Older kiddos tend to need more control over their world. To accommodate this, take them to the store and let them choose their own potty chair, or allow them to decorate one you already have with stickers. This will help them feel a connection with the potty by giving them a sense of ownership.

In most cases, it's best to start with a floor potty as opposed to using an insert for the regular toilet. A floor potty is less intimidating because it's scaled to your child's size, and they'll be able to sit on it without assistance. Right now when your child uses their diaper, they're accustomed to their pee and poop being right up against their body when they go (seems gross, I know). For some kids, when they use the potty and the pee and poop come out and *away* from their body, it can be a totally different, even scary, sensation. So with a floor potty, the pee and poop don't have as far to go.

The toilet can be scary not only from a size standpoint, but also because the splash and the sound of the flush can be big turnoffs. One bad experience on the big toilet can majorly derail any other potty training progress. But don't worry! In step 4, I'll talk about ways you can avoid this. On the other hand, if your child already has experience sitting on and using the big toilet (maybe from being at school), still incorporate that as part of your process, because it will make the transition to using the bathroom in places other than home much easier when the time comes.

Taking Your Child to the Bathroom with You

Your child probably already follows you into the bathroom at times. It could be just to ask you for a snack, not because of a general interest in what goes on in there. Either way, encouraging your child to come into the bathroom with you when you need to go is one of the easiest ways to introduce them to the concept of using the potty. Make sure you're very vocal about every little thing you're doing, starting with the initial urge to go. Say, "My belly is telling me I need to go potty!" Let them know our bodies send us signals about when it's time to go, and talk a little bit about what that feels like. Once you're in the bathroom, talk them through each step. "First, I pull down my pants and under-wear. Then I sit down on the toilet. Then I push out the pee or poop. *[Remind them that sometimes we need to wait when it comes to pooping.]* Then I get some toilet paper and wipe. Last, we flush, and wash our hands." As time goes on, you can start asking them what step comes next. Asking questions invites cooperation while testing their knowledge. Once they seem to feel comfortable, you can ask if they would like to give a doll or toy a turn, or if they would like to try the potty themselves. But don't be too pushy. If they aren't feeling it yet, that's okay. Either way, they're still learning!

Keep in mind that kids tend to make the most connection with adults who are the same sex as they are. So it can be a great learning opportunity when dads (or uncles or grandpas) take their sons in the bathroom with them (don't be too proud to sit down to pee!) and moms (or aunts or older sisters) take their daughters. It's great when your child can trust a guiding adult who can be the model for using the potty. This adult can pave the way to open dialogue and general exposure to the bathroom. The more of all these things they get, the more comfortable they'll feel when the diapers are gone.

GET YOUR CHILD ON BOARD

Once you've introduced the toilet itself to your child, and they're familiar with the steps of going potty from watching you, gently let them know they'll be using the potty soon, too. To avoid any anxiety about the impending change, it's important to demonstrate how using the potty can be fun and something to be proud of.

Children thrive on routine and schedules, so it's helpful to ease your child into the notion of no more diapers by doing a countdown on the calendar, as I briefly mentioned before. Choose three to five days before you've decided to start potty training and wake up each morning and "X" off the day on the calendar together. This is the perfect opportunity to empower your child and build their confidence, not only so they believe they can do it, but also so they realize the change is definitely coming. As you're marking off the days, say things like, "Three more days until you're a big boy!" and "You're going to look so cool in big girl underwear!" Really play up how awesome getting rid of diapers is going to be.

You also want to incorporate some fun potty-related activities into your daily routine, such as reading potty books. Most libraries have a potty training section with lots of great books, so pick up a few and pull out a different one every couple of days to keep your child engaged. Look for a mix of books, some that are silly and some that are more instructional. There are even interactive books with flaps and sounds, and these can make a big impact. Here's a fun tip: When reading to your child, change the name of the character who is using the potty to your child's name to make the story more relatable to them.

As we all know, kids love technology and screen time, so this can be an exciting and engaging way to gear your child up for potty training. Show them some potty videos or download a potty app for them to play on a mobile device. (Always check out the apps first yourself to make sure you approve of the content.) If your child has a character they're particularly fond of, try to find a video featuring that character.

While you're reading and watching videos with your little one, ask questions as you go along to keep them focused, and allow the info to really sink in. The emphasis should be more on education than on entertainment, but that doesn't need to take away from your child's pleasure in the experience. Ask things like, "How do you think [main character] feels after using the potty?" and "What do you think they should do next?" and "What do you think *you* will like best about using the potty?" You want your child to be able to find the positives in the potty training process.

One of the most effective ways to help a child learn is through play. In fact, according to Dr. Karyn Purvis of the Institute of Child

Development, "It takes an average of 400 repetitions to create a new synapse in the brain, unless it is done with play, in which case it only takes 10 to 20 repetitions." Pretty powerful stuff! As you're building your child up to no more diapers, have them practice the new skill they're learning by "teaching" a doll or toy how to use the potty. Drink and wet dolls work great for this and can really help your child comprehend the mechanics of the human body. Some are even anatomically correct and come with miniature potty chairs. They can get kind of pricey, and you can get the same results using any doll or toy that your child already has. Just substitute a small bowl for the toy potty.

Kids have great imaginations, so run with it! Pretend to give the doll something to drink and make it do a little "potty dance." Ask your child, "What do you think the dolly needs to do?" You're guiding them to say, "Go potty!" (If they don't, you can help them along). Have the doll sit on the potty and pretend to relieve itself. You can even sneak a couple chocolate chips in the potty to mimic poop if you're feeling extra creative. Your child can wipe the doll and help it get dressed. Then really celebrate the doll's success! Throw a little party with treats, singing, and dancing. Tell the doll how proud you are of it for using the potty. Let your child know that if they go on the potty, they'll get a treat, too. Playing this game is sure to get your child excited to use the potty.

REWARDS

Using rewards is one of the best ways to reinforce good potty behavior. There are children who love to do things simply to make others happy—to them, seeing a positive reaction and hearing praise is enough. However, most children, especially as they get older, aren't motivated to do things unless there's something in it for them. Whether it be their favorite piece of candy, a very small toy, or a sticker, getting that tangible reward gives them the incentive to do it and to do it again. Every child has a motivator; you just need to find out what it is.

Whatever you choose, the reward should possess the following characteristics:

- **It should be immediate.** Young children don't always have the ability to process things to come in the future, which is why sticker charts that build toward future rewards aren't always effective, especially with younger kids. Giving the reward immediately following the success ingrains in your child that the behavior they just did is correct.

- **It should be exclusive.** It really helps if you're able to find something new that your child has never had before and to keep that reward *only* for potty success. If you're offering them a special candy for using the potty, but they also get that candy for completing other tasks, like finishing their meal or sleeping in their bed all night, they could end up waiting until those other times to get the candy, derailing your potty progress.

- **It should be consistent.** Remember, your child loves knowing what to expect, so keep the reward the same for each type of potty success. Even if your child seems to have forgotten about the reward and doesn't ask for it, offer it anyway. They'll appreciate that you kept your promise.

A Sticker Chart

A sticker chart is a great tool to incorporate into your potty repertoire. This isn't the kind of sticker chart that earns future rewards. Rather, the sticker itself is part of the reward. Every time your child has success on the potty, let them choose a sticker and put it on their chart. Most children are visual learners, and the chart really allows them to *see* their progress. Hang the chart on the refrigerator or in a central location of the home. At the end of each day, show them the chart and celebrate together as a family. Being able to visualize all their successes in one place will give your child a huge confidence boost and can inspire them to get more stickers the next day.

Candy

This is probably the first thing every parent's mind goes to when thinking of rewards. Candy can be a great reward option, especially if your child doesn't typically get it otherwise. If you go this route, keep in mind that your child will be using the potty multiple times a day. Keep the treat small so you don't regret the decision. Your child generally won't care about the size or quantity of the treat, just that they get it in general. Also, too much sugar can lead to constipation or disrupted sleep, and either could end up hindering your progress.

Toys

If your child doesn't have a sweet tooth (lucky you!), or if you would rather not resort to candy, small toys are also a great motivator. The toy doesn't need to be anything expensive or fancy. Go to the dollar store and choose several items your child would like. To add to the excitement, wrap each toy like a gift and display them all in a basket in the bathroom (keep it out of your child's reach), and then allow them to choose a gift to unwrap with each potty success.

Verbal and Physical Praise

Even though tangible rewards such as toys and candy are typically the best motivators for most children, there should be no shortage of verbal praise, hugs, kisses, and high fives, as well. Say things like, "It makes me so happy when you pee or poop on the potty!" or "I like it when you pee or poop on the potty!" or "You just used the potty like a big kid!" Be specific when praising, so your child really makes the connection as to what behavior is expected of them. Another fun idea is to make up a potty song and dance to do together every time your child has success. The sillier the better! Kids love to see their parents act like goofballs.

New, Fun Undies

To help your child feel included in the changes that come along with potty training, take them to the store and let them choose their own cool, new underwear featuring their favorite character, design, or colors. They'll probably try a little harder not to pee on a superhero, unicorn, or rainbow.

SCRIPT

Having your child keep you company in the bathroom is a great way for them to see there's nothing scary going on in there. You can use the following lines to help your child get comfortable with the idea of using the potty. Shape your dialogues to encourage your individual child.

"Can you read me a story while I go potty?"

"Let's explore the bathroom. Do you know what the potty is for? It's where we put our pee and poop."

"Mommy's belly feels a little funny. I need to go potty! I'm going to put all my pee in the potty now."

"I think your dolly needs to go potty! Can you show her what to do?"

"I see you've got the wiggles. What do you think that means? It's your body telling you to go potty!"

LEARN TO READ YOUR CHILD'S SIGNS

I hate to say it, but your child most likely isn't going to verbally self-initiate or communicate that they need to go potty at first. Therefore, it's important that you know what signals to look for so you can get them to the potty at the appropriate times. This is going to be a learning curve, because, until now, you probably haven't paid too much attention to your child's "potty language." When they were in diapers, you had no reason to. Most of us don't realize that it's actually pretty apparent how our children behave when they need to use the potty. Every child has at least one cue, as subtle as it may be. By taking some time to observe these behaviors, you'll proactively be able to turn potential accidents into successes once you start potty training.

Grabbing Genitals

This is one of the most telling signs. Your child is experiencing a sensation down there, and they aren't quite sure what to make of it. They touch, thinking it will make the sensation go away, kind of like how when we hurt ourselves, our first instinct is to grab the injured area. When you see this, say, "It looks like you need to use the potty! Come on, let's go sit." Be careful with overprompting though. Some kids might do this even when they don't need to use the potty!

Squatting

A lot of children prefer a squatting position, especially for pooping. It feels more natural and requires less straining. Be on the lookout for this kind of positioning, and if your child only poops while squatting, you definitely want to start off with a small potty as close to the floor as possible to mimic that position for them. If they still seem to struggle, let them put their feet up on a small step stool.

Fidgeting

Some children can get very antsy, even hyperactive, when they need to use the bathroom. Hence the term, "the wiggles" or "the potty dance." They wait so long that it can cause them to act out and not be able to focus properly. If your child tends to show this type of behavior, you will need to prompt them to sit on the potty more frequently to avoid it. Even though it's obvious that they need to go, it can actually be harder to convince them to use the potty when they've gotten to this point, which can be frustrating for everybody involved.

Hiding

Children hide, particularly when pooping, out of a desire for privacy. When you see your child sneaking away to hide, try to redirect them to the potty instead. Once you're able to get them to sit (even if you have to use a distraction of some sort), pretend that you forgot something in the other room and step away for a minute, or wrap a blanket around them. Once their need for privacy is satisfied, they'll feel comfortable enough to release.

Crossing Legs

When your child crosses their legs, it's their way of trying to "hold it." They usually will do this because they're involved in something and don't want to stop to use the potty. Try to remember that your child is used to the convenience of just going in their diaper whenever the urge strikes. The FOMO (fear of missing out) struggle is very real with toddlers! If your child is resistant to a gentle prompt, allow them to take whatever they're playing with to the potty, or "press" an imaginary pause button to freeze the activity. Doing this will help them feel like they aren't going to miss anything.

Passing Gas

Most children will pass gas more frequently when they need to poop. If you notice your little stinker doing this, say, "Do you smell that? It *smells* like you need to go potty. Come on, let's go try." Since smell is more tangible than just a feeling, it can be a great way for your child to make the connection that their body is trying to tell them they need to poop. A helpful tip: Once you get your child to sit on the potty, if the poop doesn't come, ask them to try to pass gas again. They could very well push the poop out along with it!

Potty Anxiety

Some children can have fear or anxiety about using the potty. In this case, signals that your child needs to go include being extra clingy, whining, lack of appetite, and a sudden loss of interest in things they typically enjoy. Do your best to comfort them, don't be too pushy with prompting, and try to distract them with something fun. It doesn't necessarily mean they aren't ready; it just means they need a little extra love and encouragement.

TROUBLESHOOTING TECHNIQUES

I can't tell when my child is peeing or pooping in their diaper.

Some children are "stealth poopers." The best way to address this is to try a little naked time, with nothing on their bottom at all so you can see them going as soon as it starts (more on this in step 3). Before you panic and intervene, first take note of signs like their position and facial expression, and see if you're able to nail down one sign to help give you clues in the future.

My child sits on the potty for long periods, but never does anything!

It's great that your child will sit on the potty without resistance! But it can become a problem if the potty becomes their new favorite seat for snack time or movie night. Try limiting the time your child sits on the potty to when it's likely they actually need to go. If they sit but don't go within a set time frame (usually three minutes for pee and 10 minutes for poop), have them get up, and redirect them to a different place to sit. This will help them make the connection that the potty is only for peeing and pooping. Additionally, if you've been offering rewards for sitting on the potty, it's time to up the ante and give the treat only for actually using it!

How do I get rid of rewards once I start?

Some children will stop asking for treats when they use the potty on their own, so you can just follow their lead in this case. However, some kids are going to milk it for as long as they possibly can. Obviously, you don't want to give them a treat every time they go potty for the next year, but at the same time, you don't want to suddenly cut off rewards and risk backtracking on any progress they've made. Wait for your little one to be using the potty consistently for at least a week or two, and then start to set longer term goals for them. Instead of rewarding every individual potty success, shoot for every good potty *day*. When you increase the goal, increase the reward. For example, replace one candy for each pee in the potty with one TV show and a small bowl of frozen yogurt after dinner for a full day with no accidents. Move toward each successful week, then month, and then phase out the rewards altogether.

My child isn't motivated by tangible rewards like treats or toys.

If this is the case, try using an experience such as watching a movie or TV show, baking cookies together, or a trip to the playground. Often, the effect of an experience can resonate more, and it doesn't lose its novelty as easily as candy or toys might. This can be especially true if you don't always get a lot of time to spend together.

STEP 2 RECAP: FIVE TAKEAWAYS

1. Introduce the potty as early as possible. The more familiar your child is with the bathroom and what it's for, the less anxious and afraid they'll be when it's time to start potty training.

2. Make potty training fun by reading books, watching videos, and playing games. Allow your child to feel in control by letting them choose their own underwear, and decorate their potty

with stickers. You want potty training to be something your child looks forward to, not something they dread.

3. Rewards are a great way to accelerate potty training progress. Find something your child likes, and use that as a motivator to get the potty behavior you're aiming for.

4. In addition to using rewards, be generous with verbal and physical praise, too. It's very important that your child understands you're proud of them and that they should be proud of themselves.

5. Learn to read your child's potty language so you can turn potential accidents into learning opportunities. You can start observing your child's cues even before you start the potty training process so you'll know what to look for once the diapers are off.

STEP 3
Say Bye-bye, Diapers!

GREAT JOB ON ALL THE TIME YOU'VE PUT IN getting your child pumped up for potty training! Now it's finally time to dive in and ditch those diapers!* This will be the only portion of the process that should be condensed into one set time frame. Choose a weekend, a day, or an evening (however much time you can spare) when you'll be able to focus on your child and their potty behaviors.

* Before you get started at home, always check in with your child's caregivers or daycare staff regarding their potty training policies and practices to ensure you can keep things as consistent as possible across the board. (Full details on this in step 4.)

During this time, you'll be watching for your child's patterns and cues, which means no distractions! Make sure the time you choose does not involve events or visitors. You want things to be as normal as possible to provide a comfortable and consistent learning environment. Since you'll mostly be at home, at least for the initial period (no matter how short), try to plan some fun activities to do with your child so you aren't just sitting around waiting for an accident. You may have lost the diapers, but you don't need to lose your sanity along with them!

THINGS YOU'LL NEED

Before you officially start, there are some supplies you'll want to have on hand that will make the potty training process run smoothly. Depending on your child's personality, consider taking them shopping for these items with you to help get them excited about the process!

- **Potty chair:** Having at least one small floor potty is very important for many reasons. As I mentioned in step 2, it's much less intimidating than the actual toilet because of its small size, and because your child can easily get on and off on their own. Its portable nature also allows you to keep it with you wherever you happen to be in the house, so you won't be confined to the bathroom. Plus, when you're ready to take the show on the road, the potty can easily be kept in the car for emergencies.

- **Rewards:** Make sure to have plenty of your reward of choice on hand before you start potty training. Also, gather the materials needed to make a progress chart (items like construction paper, markers, and stickers). It can even be fun for you and your child to make the chart together!

- **Flushable wipes:** These are a potty training staple because they clean better and are less messy than toilet paper, making it easier for your child to wipe themselves. Also, regular baby wipes should never be flushed. (Even with flushable wipes, take care to not flush more than one or two at a time to avoid plumbing issues.)

- **Dedicated potty activity** (at least one): Get a few new books, a coloring pad, or a magnetic drawing board to keep in a basket next to the potty, or download a new game on your mobile device. Whatever you choose, it should be something that your child doesn't normally have access to, so that its exclusivity to potty time will motivate them to go!

- **Underwear:** It's a good idea to have at least two or three packs of underwear on hand so you can introduce them when you're ready. At first, buy them a size too big. Snug-fitting underwear can easily be confused with the feeling of a diaper!

Steps 1 and 2 covered how to best prepare yourself and your child. You're also going to benefit from preparing your home. Let's face it, potty training can be downright messy at times, and you're busy enough without having to shampoo your carpets when it's all said and done! Roll up area rugs and protect furniture with towels or, better yet, waterproof mattress pads (many times these will stay nice and secure over couch cushions!). Also, have some good stain remover on hand, just in case.

> **Parent hack:** Placing soiled rugs or cushions in direct sunlight to dry after cleaning takes away that stubborn urine smell!

DITCHING THE DIAPERS

This is the moment you've been building up to for the past few days or weeks. You're about to officially start potty training—how exciting! You might be feeling a little nervous, which is totally normal, but remember to maintain an air of positivity and confidence. Your little one is going to be looking to you for reassurance during this new adventure. Since you most likely don't have a long block of time all at once to spend on potty training, it's important to make the most of every moment. Try to be as hands-on as possible, so you can keep your child engaged with you, making it easier to watch for patterns and to get them to the potty at the appropriate times.

When trying to incorporate potty training into an already busy lifestyle, you may find there are portions of this step that you need to go back and repeat a few times before your child is a potty pro—and that's perfectly okay! Remember, potty training is a marathon, not a sprint.

(Note: Information pertaining to naptime, nighttime, and poop training can be a little different, and I'll be covering those topics specifically in step 5.)

Say Bye-bye, Diapers!

This event should be ceremonial. Take this opportunity to really empower your child. Tell them that today is a very special day because they're officially becoming a big kid! Have them remove their diaper and throw it in the garbage themselves while saying, "Bye-bye, diapers!" This event is so important because the physical act of throwing away their diaper signifies the start of something new, making it easier for your child to process than just being told their diapers are gone. If they need further confirmation, put all the diapers away in a closet (or somewhere your child won't find them), show them the empty spot where their diapers once were, and say, "See, no more diapers! We need to put our pee and poop in the potty now." Make a big deal about how proud you are of them, show them their potty, and let them know that is where they're going to try to put their pee and poop today.

To avoid any nerves or anxiety, you want to be supportive by telling them you'll be by their side helping them learn. It can be helpful to do an initial practice potty run at this point, so your child will know what to expect when it comes time to go. And don't forget to remind them of the pending reward, to build excitement and for extra motivation!

From there, get started with some of the fun you have planned for the day. Have a loose schedule of activities broken down by pre-nap/lunch and post-nap/lunch, so you can avoid downtime. The idea is to keep your child as engaged with you as possible, so you're able to keep an eye on their potty language and redirect them to the potty at the appropriate times. (I'll be covering the best times to take your child to the potty in the next section). Take care to not put too much pressure on your child about using the potty. Make the potty learning seem secondary to the special one-on-one time you have planned. I always say if you're working hard to make your child happy, they're more likely to work hard to make you happy by using the potty correctly!

To make the most of your time, and to ensure your child gets as much practice as possible, keep a drink in their hand throughout the day. The more they drink, the more they'll need to pee! And it will also keep them hydrated to prevent constipation. If your child isn't a big drinker, feed them a salty snack, which will help them feel thirsty. Just be sure to avoid too much sugary juice and soda because those drinks can lead to unruly behavior or disrupted sleep—neither of which you need to deal with in your already busy schedule!

Going Commando

Diaper-free potty training is the most effective way to see results quickly. Once your child throws their diaper away, don't put anything back on at first. You can either keep them completely naked, just bottomless, or in a dress or long shirt with nothing underneath.

Avoid jumping straight into underwear on the first day. Until now, your child hasn't needed to think about peeing or pooping before they just let it out. They've had their bottom covered (except for diaper changes and bath time) since moments after birth, so it can be challenging for them to make the distinction between underwear and a diaper in the very beginning. Being bottomless is a very important body-awareness activity because it makes it more apparent to your child when they are peeing or pooping and that there is no longer something there to catch the mess when they go. It also makes it easier for them to get to the potty quickly on their own, without having to fumble with pulling off clothing. Just as important, it helps *you* be more aware of when they start going and gives you the opportunity to catch your child in time to turn the accident into a success.

If you're somehow able to spend more than two days in a row on potty training, you won't want your child to stay completely bottomless any longer than the first day and a half. One of the most common potty training dilemmas parents face can be making the transition from naked or commando to underwear. If your child goes naked for longer than one and a half to two days in a row, you run the risk of having a child who's potty trained *only* when they're naked, which is not super helpful considering it isn't socially acceptable to be naked in public! For the average child, a day and a half of being bottomless is the perfect amount of time to allow them to learn how to recognize their body signals, to solidify that the diapers are gone, and to show their messes will be messes if they have an accident.

TO THE POTTY!

Okay, so you've taken off the diapers. Now, how exactly do you get the pee and poop into the potty? You have a few options here, and I'm going to describe them all for you, so you can decide what you think will work best for your situation. If you find one isn't working, go ahead and give another a try. This can take some experimentation. When you find one that works, don't flip-flop around beyond that to avoid confusing your child. Consistency is going to be key to your little one achieving success.

As hard as it is to resist getting caught up in those adorable little butt cheeks running around, you want to be paying extra attention to your child's cues and potty language. Remember everything you've learned from the recon you've been doing up to this point. You want to keep the potty within arm's reach wherever you happen to be so you can move into action fast. No matter how prepared you might feel, in the beginning there will probably be at least one occasion when you don't notice until it's too late and your child has already started going. But that's actually a good thing! I'm sure you're thinking, *Okay crazy lady, how can that be good?* It's good because it's almost a guarantee that you can get some pee or poop into the potty! And pee or poop in the potty equals learning and success!

A soon as you notice your child starting to go, don't freeze—get them onto that potty as soon as possible! It can be easy to over-react and freak out a little when that happens, but try your best to calmly transfer them onto the potty to finish. It's good to ver-balize what's happening, "Look, you're peeing! Let's get to the potty." Potty training can be a comedy of errors, so don't be afraid to laugh at the situation. It will end up making everyone, espe-cially your child, feel more at ease. In these scenarios, if *any* pee or poop makes it into the potty, even just a drop, you should praise and reward your child as if they had gone there in the first place. Use lots of verbal praise, hugs, and high fives, let them choose a sticker and put it on their progress chart, and give them their treat or reward.

Any time there's potty success, have your child help you empty the contents of the potty into the toilet and flush it away. Make it even more of a game by saying, "Bye-bye, poopy!" Not only is this fun for your child to participate in, but also it helps aid in the transition from potty to regular toilet by letting them see nothing scary happens once their pee and poop goes in.

Bathroom Reminders

Since using the potty is such a new experience for your child, they're going to need some reminders about when to go. Depend-ing on your child's personality and the way they learn, you can choose one or a combination of the following methods to encour-age potty use.

- **Prompting:** Prompting is one very effective way to let your child know it's time to use the potty. Appropriate times to prompt are when you notice your child hasn't gone in a while, when it's a normal time that they usually go (for poop especially), or when they have an obvious case of the wiggles. It's very important to note the distinction between prompting and asking. You don't necessarily want to **ask** your child if they need to go potty, mainly because they're likely to answer with every young child's favorite word: No! Plus, almost no new potty trainee is going to want to voluntarily stop whatever activity they're in the middle of to go sit on the potty, and they may not even fully recognize the feeling of needing to go just yet.

In the beginning, it's much more effective to **tell** your child it's potty time instead of just asking them. But you want to be careful that you aren't nagging or prompting too often. You don't want your child to get annoyed by the process. Give them a little bit of space. If your child is really resistant to your prompt, it most likely means they really don't need to go. Instead of insisting, just let them know that they can try after a few more minutes.

- **Timers:** Using a timer instead of prompting can also be very productive. You can simply set a timer on your phone or smart speaker, or you can get your child a wrist timer or potty watch to wear. This is the best technique if you have other responsibilities you're trying to take care of at the same time, like caring for a younger child or working from home. A good rule of thumb is to start with every 30 minutes, then move to every 60 minutes, and finally to every 90 minutes as you notice your child's control improving, but feel free to make adjustments as needed. Let your child know that once the timer goes off, it means it's time to sit on the potty whether or not they think they need to go. Timers are also a good alternative for those children who aren't super receptive to being told what to do. The sense of independence and responsibility your child gets from the timer helps them feel like they're in control of the situation.

- **Child-led:** If your child is one of those more stubborn kiddos who doesn't respond well to prompting or timers, you'll just need to step back and let them know to tell you when they need to go, or wait for them to start going and then transfer them to the potty to finish. Your child may be more receptive to being given a choice and respond well to a question like, "Do you want to sit on the potty before or after you brush your teeth?" This takes away the opportunity for outright refusal and gives them a certain level of control over the situation. Some children need everything to be their idea, and you don't ever want to force them to sit on the potty, or they could start to resent the process.

SCRIPT

You can use any or all of the following lines and adapt them to your style. They'll help you get your child motivated to get to the potty, and to get there in time.

"Now that your diapers are off, your pee and poop go in the potty."

"Look, you're peeing! Let's get to the potty!"

"I see you have the wiggles, what do you think that means? It means you need to go potty!" By giving your child the option to answer a question instead of just telling them what to do, it comes across as teamwork instead of a command.

Use simple prompts such as "Come on, it's time to sit on the potty," instead of asking a yes-or-no question like "Do you need to go potty?"

"Oops, you had an accident. Remember pee and poop go only in the potty now, not on the floor or in your pants."

REDIRECTION

As a busy parent, you're trying to balance multiple responsibilities while potty training. When you first start, and even throughout the process, you won't be able to catch them all—accidents are bound to happen. Dealing with accidents is without question the most frustrating part of potty training. But know that they're a completely normal part of the learning process! Every child makes mistakes when learning a new skill. It's very important to be patient and not allow any personal frustration to show. Many people tend to keep track of the number of accidents during potty training as a way to gauge progress, but really you should only be keeping track of the successes.

In the very beginning, accidents are simply because your child doesn't yet possess the muscle control or awareness to make it to the potty in time. Once your child starts to understand the concept, accidents can still occur, and most of the time they're a result of distraction. If your child is engrossed in an activity, like playing outside, two things tend to occur. Number one, they're less aware of the sensation of needing to go potty until it starts happening, and number two, they'll hold it in so they don't have to stop the activity, potentially until it's too late. Accidents are also more likely to occur when your child is sick, very tired, or overly excited.

Whenever your child says they need to use the potty, do your best to take them right away. When you first scrap the diapers, the time between your child realizing they need to go and the pee or poop actually coming out is only about 10 to 15 seconds, so you want to make sure you avoid the accident if possible. That way you can reward your child for three behaviors: recognizing their need to go, letting you know in time, and using the potty successfully!

Solutions

No matter the reason for the accident, there should never be any shaming, scolding, or punishing. At the same time, you don't necessarily want to be *too* comforting either, because that could actually make your child falsely believe that accidents are acceptable. A minimal, matter-of-fact reaction works best. If you aren't able to catch any pee or poop in the potty once the accident starts, quickly acknowledge the situation by saying, "Oops, you peed on the floor. Remember, pee goes only in the potty now. Let's try harder to get there next time. Just tell me and I can help you." (You can use any combination of these statements).

When there is an accident, even if you think there's nothing left to come out, it's important to sit your child on the potty afterward as they may not have finished peeing or pooping. If they get anything in the potty at that point, still treat it as a success. Put most of your focus and attention on your child's positive potty behaviors and not as much on the negatives.

To avoid accidents when you're out and about, always encourage your child to use the potty before you leave and then again when you get to where you're going. Many children will say, "No, I don't have to go," but then will need to go at the least opportune time, such as when you're stuck in traffic on your way to drop them off at daycare. If you notice this to be true with your child, it's helpful to incorporate potty use into your daily out-the-door routine. Add using the potty to a short list of other tasks you direct your child to do. For example, you could say, "Please use the potty, put your shoes on, and say goodbye to Mommy." Always make sure to praise and/or reward their compliance.

If you find the accidents are persistent and you aren't seeing any improvement, it can help to exaggerate the cleanup process as much as possible. Make your child stop playing until everything is cleaned up, and do a thorough wipe-down or bathe them before changing their clothes. This shows your child that using the potty is faster than going in their pants or on the floor. You can also have them participate in the cleanup if you think that would be a deterrent based on your child's personality. If you decide to try this tactic, remember it should not be used as a form of punishment, but rather as an automatic and consistent result to the behavior.

Occasionally some children will have small dribbles in their underwear before making it to the potty, not even enough to penetrate through to make their pants wet. This is normal and shouldn't be considered an accident. It's your child's way of testing the limits to see how long they can go before stopping and getting to the potty. Remind them to stop and go as soon as they feel the need. As their muscle control improves, this behavior will diminish.

TROUBLESHOOTING TECHNIQUES

My child is very attached to their diapers, and I'm worried they'll be upset about throwing them away.
If diapers are important to your little one, then just throwing them away in the garbage may not be the best option for you. To your child, those familiar white things that have been securely wrapped around them holding their pee and poop aren't just trash, so treat the diapers with a little more respect. Have your child help you box them up and wrap them like a gift, and then you can leave it on the front porch for the "mail carrier" to take to another family that needs them more.

Scenario 1. My household is very traditional, so bottomless is not an option for us. Scenario 2. My child is very uncomfortable being naked/bottomless.

If you or your child is *really* opposed to being bottomless, or if it just isn't an option for you for any reason (maybe it happens to be really cold wherever you are, or maybe you rent an apartment with all white carpet), that's okay! You can keep your child in very loose basketball shorts or a dress with nothing underneath so their bottom is concealed. (Or your child may feel more comfortable and/or warmer wearing long socks.) If you have nice weather, take the show outside! That way if you have any accidents, there is nothing to clean up except your child.

My child refuses to sit on the potty!

This can be very frustrating, but it's important to remember that this whole potty training experience is very new (and maybe even a little scary) for your child. If your child refuses to sit on the potty, that obviously makes it very difficult to potty train! You can warm your child up to sitting on their potty by showing their favorite doll or toy or a sibling sitting on it, or allowing them to pour water into the potty so they can see that when something goes in, nothing scary happens. Above all, take baby steps and do your best to use patience and reassurance to comfort your child's uneasiness.

My child sits on the potty, but nothing comes out!

First, put yourself in their shoes. Imagine if someone told you no more peeing and pooping on the toilet and to do it in a diaper instead. It would be hard for you to make that transition, right? So, if your child sits on the potty but doesn't release, your time may be better invested in just waiting for them to start going and then sitting them on the potty to finish. Once they see that they can do it a couple of times (even if it takes a little help from you), they'll feel more comfortable doing it on their own. Also, having your child blow bubbles or take deep breaths, turning on the tap (for the sound of running water), or placing your child's feet in a bowl of warm water are all effective tricks to encourage release!

CHARTING PROGRESS

As I've already mentioned, it's important to pay attention to and learn your child's cues, behaviors, and potty language. You probably have a pretty good handle on all that at this point. But it's also going to be very valuable to jot these and other things down as you're working with your child so that when you go back to your regular routine, the transition is as seamless as possible when your child is in someone else's care. Things that you want to make note of include how much liquid your child drinks before needing to use the potty, how often your child tends to go potty (both pee and poop), and how long they're able to hold their bladder. You'll also want to note changes to their behavior when they need to use the potty and particulars about their potty preferences. It will make everyone's lives much easier when you have it all written down in one place, like on the handy progress chart you can find on page 100.

How Much Liquid Your Child Drinks Before Needing to Go to the Bathroom

You can gauge this by noting when you give your child something to drink, the approximate volume (don't get out a measuring cup or anything!), how long it takes them to finish the drink, and any times they use the bathroom in between. This important information will allow your child's caregivers to prompt them to use the potty at appropriate times, especially if your child isn't to the point of self-initiation just yet.

How Many Times per Hour Your Child Needs to Pee

The easiest thing to do is to jot down each time your child pees over the first few days of potty training. Based on that, you should be able to see somewhat of a trend. You can pass this information on to your child's caregivers, so they'll know how often they should be prompting potty use, even if it differs some between mornings and afternoons. If things seem a bit all over the place (which it very well might at first), a general rule of thumb is every 30 minutes. But as your child gets further into the potty training process, the time in between pees will gradually increase.

How Often Your Child Poops

There are two important things to note when it comes to poop timing: frequency (or number of poops per day) and time of day (i.e., first thing in the morning, mid-morning, lunchtime, evening, etc.). Most children are at least somewhat predictable when it comes to their poop timing and habits. However, keep in mind that during potty training, poop frequency naturally decreases. No one is really sure why, but it does certainly make things more convenient. Your twice-a-day pooper may go down to once a day or even every other day. And that is totally normal. Pass along your child's poop signals, schedule, and habits, so the caregiver can be on higher alert during those times.

How Long Your Child Can Hold Their Bladder

By "hold their bladder," I mean how long they can go from the time they indicate needing to use the potty until the pee actually comes. In the beginning, it's almost instantaneous, so your caregiver will need to take them to the potty as soon as they see your child's potty dance or as soon as your child says they need to go. But as the training process progresses, your child's control will increase, and you'll start to be able to ask them if they can wait to go until you have access to the potty for them.

How Your Child's Behavior Changes When They Need to Use the Potty

By now you should have a pretty good grasp of how your child's behavior can indicate their need to go potty. Most children get antsy, lose the ability to listen or focus, or act out when they really need to use the bathroom. Write down things your caregiver can look for instead of just waiting for your child to communicate their need verbally.

Your Child's Potty Preferences

Include in your instructions to your child's caregiver things your child tends to do or enjoys doing while on the potty, so the caregiver can carry over the same activities consistently in the new environment. Examples include: singing a certain song while sitting on the potty, using a small potty as opposed to the regular toilet, reading a particular book while they sit, and receiving certain rewards and reactions to their success. By maintaining these same practices even when your child is not in your care, they're sure to feel more comfortable using the potty in a different place.

STEP 3 RECAP: FIVE TAKEAWAYS

1. Gather the essential potty training items you need before you get started. These include a potty chair, any rewards you've chosen, cool new underwear for after the switch, flushable wipes, a dedicated potty activity, and cleaning supplies in case of accidents.

2. Involve and empower your child by ceremoniously saying goodbye to their diapers. You want to avoid having them jump straight into underwear. Give your child a little naked/bottomless time so they can more quickly become familiar with the sensations of needing to go potty.

3. To help ensure success, keep the potty within arm's reach of wherever you happen to be. If you notice cues that your child needs to go or if they start to have an accident, you can get them onto the potty as quickly as possible.

4. Accidents are going to happen and that's okay! Mistakes are an important part of the learning process. As frustrating as it may be, do your best to focus only on the successes!

5. There are some important things you want to jot down, such as how long before your child goes potty after drinking, how many times they go per day, and how often. That way, when it's time to hand off potty training to another caregiver, there's a plan in place to keep everything as consistent as possible for your child.

STEP 4
Back to Real Life

ONCE YOU'VE COMPLETED STEP 3 at least once, feel free to go back to your normal schedule. If you normally work, go back to work. If your child goes to a grandparent or daycare, send them back to their grandparent or daycare. I don't want you to be held hostage by potty training! Potty training should fit into your daily routine, not the other way around.

I'm not by any means suggesting your child should be fully potty trained at this point—remember that it could take a few times going through the motions to get all the way there. You may even find that you need to keep your child in cloth or disposable trainers when with a caregiver in order to comply with the caregiver's rules and policies, while your kiddo is diaper free at home. Cloth training pants can be a great tool for a busy parent because they feel less like diapers and help keep your child aware of any accidents while still containing the mess. They also help avoid any confusion for your child ("I thought she said no more diapers?"), while keeping the expectation clear that pee and poop go only in the potty now.

Making the choice to go diaper-free full time can be a difficult one. But the good news is you've already done a lot of the hard work! In this step, I'm going to cover taking your child outside, and how to hand off potty training to another caregiver, including daycare specifically, so you can keep the process as consistent as possible for your child while maintaining or advancing their progress.

TAKING YOUR CHILD OUTSIDE

I completely understand that you may need to run errands or leave the house at some point during potty training. First, don't panic! This is actually going to be a great way to test the waters and learn how your little one will do once back in an environment with distractions and different stimuli. They need to be potty trained both in *and* out of the house, after all! In fact, by the afternoon of day two (if you're able to spend a full weekend working on step 3), I recommend one short outing. You want to keep it low-key (think grocery store or library, not bounce house or birthday party) and within 30 minutes from home.

What to Bring

As hard as it will be, resist the urge to go back to diapers or disposable trainers, and keep your child in loose pants or shorts with nothing underneath for the first few trips out of the house. Try to make sure they use the potty before leaving, and turn your diaper bag into a "potty training survival kit." Pack at least two sets of clean clothes, a plastic bag to put wet clothes in, wipes for cleaning your child, and at least one cloth diaper/burp cloth/absorbent cloth to wipe up any mess that might get somewhere other than on your child, like on the floor of Aisle 9 in a superstore. Also don't forget to pack a spare pair of socks and shoes—pee has nowhere to go but down! If it isn't winter, you could just keep your child in flip-flops or plastic clogs, which are easily rinsed off and put back on. You might even want to consider keeping a clean shirt for yourself, just in case (I speak from experience here). And remember to bring whatever rewards you were using at home along with you to maintain consistent results for good potty behavior.

Portable Potties

You'll also find it beneficial to keep a potty with you in your travels. You have a few options in this regard. The easiest choice is to bring the potty you've been using at home along with you, or if you have a car, you can get an identical one that can stay in the car to save time. Not only is this quick and easy, but it also keeps things consistent for your child, and they'll feel most comfortable going on the potty they're used to, especially early on. The downsides to this scenario will be having to clean out the potty, or possibly having to leave wherever you are to run out to the car for a potty pit stop.

For more portability, and if a car isn't part of your life, you can purchase a portable stand-alone potty with legs that fold out and a bag that fastens to the bottom for easy clean up. If your child prefers using the toilet instead of a potty, bring along their toilet insert for comfort, or you can purchase a portable insert which folds into a small, flat package that can easily fit inside a purse or diaper bag. This last option is the least bulky and the most discreet.

Regardless of what you choose, be sure to let your child know that if they need to go potty to just let you know because you have a solution for them. Remember, this is the first time they're venturing out without the comfort of their diapers! Not only will the open communication ease their worries, but it will also give them confidence, so they won't feel like they need to hold it for too long and risk having an accident.

Car Rides

Let's face it, there's nothing worse than having to disassemble a car seat and clean it. (How can there be so many nooks and crannies in one item?) To prevent having to deal with this as a result of a potential potty accident, you can purchase washable, waterproof car seat protectors that will still allow the straps and buckles to function properly. These can also be easily transferred between car seats in grandparents' vehicles or taxis. Don't use towels, puppy pads, or anything else that could potentially compromise the safety of the car seat's functionality.

Regarding public transport, like on the plane, train, bus, or subway, for example, have your child sit on a waterproof pad (such as a puppy or hospital pad) with a hand towel over the top. Obviously, it isn't as easy to just "pull over" in the case of emergencies here, so you may be more inclined to use cloth training pants in this case for added absorbency. Still, ask your child to tell you if they need to go, but if they do and you aren't able to make it to the bathroom in time, you can still praise them for trying and let them know the accident wasn't their fault.

In any case, try to keep each leg of your journey under 30 minutes when possible, and incorporate stops periodically so your child can use the potty. If your child is resistant to trying when they might not feel the urge to go right that second, it's helpful if you offer them a small bribe (something smaller than the reward for actual potty success) for just sitting and trying.

Public Toilets

Some children will be averse to using public bathrooms at first. And understandably so. Even as an adult, I try to avoid them if at all possible! Take a step back and look at the situation through your child's eyes. So many strange sights and smells, cold hard surfaces, toilets that will flush at the drop of a hat, and hand dryers fit to send rockets into space. Try to be patient and let your child ease into public restroom use at their own pace. Start by exploring bathrooms in places other than home, like at a family member's house, for example. Gradually move to venues with smaller bathrooms (preferably single stall), and then progress from there. Whenever you get to a place other than home, point out to your child where the bathrooms are and ask them to tell you if they need to go. Children don't always assume there are bathrooms in other places, so some reassurance from you will make them less likely to have an accident. But always have a backup option to offer just in case, such as the potty in the car or the portable insert, so your child doesn't feel helpless.

> **Parent hack:** Keep a pad of "magic" sticky notes with you, so you can block the sensor on the automatic flusher to avoid a potentially traumatizing public bathroom experience!

PASSING THE BATON

Since we all have other responsibilities, at some point, your child is going to be under the care of someone other than you. And most likely, this person has not been very closely involved in your child's potty training so far. Or perhaps one parent potty trains on Saturday, and the other takes over on Sunday. Then maybe a nanny, grandparent, or daycare provider steps in on Monday. In order to maintain the potty training progress your child is making at home, it's going to be very important to keep continuity between caregivers as much as possible. If your child is diaper free while they're with you, but Grandma puts them in a diaper as soon as you pull out of the driveway, then all bets are off! It won't be fair to expect your child to be able to understand that they're supposed to put their pee and poop in the potty when they're with you, but they don't have to when they're at Grandma's house.

Planning Ahead

I always recommend speaking with your child's caregivers *before* you even start potty training. Not only does it give the caregiver time to prepare for the upcoming changes, but it also allows you to learn of any special situations, rules, or policies that you may need to take into account in your own training process. For example, if your child goes to the home of a friend who also takes care of a baby who is just learning to crawl, they most likely will have a "no accident" policy simply for hygienic reasons. Or perhaps your elderly grandmother keeps your child after school, but she isn't strong enough to lift your child up onto the toilet if needed. If you think about possible scenarios in advance, you can prepare yourself and avoid any unforeseen setbacks. (I cover information specific to daycare in the next section.)

Sharing Information

Once you have everything sorted out, write it down! Remember that handy progress chart (page 100) in the back of the book I mentioned in the previous step? This will be all the information that will allow you to maintain consistency with your child's potty routine even across multiple caregivers. Each caregiver should be aware of your child's potty signs and cues, how much liquid they can drink before going to the bathroom, poop schedules, how frequently they tend to pee, and how long they can hold their bladder. You definitely also want to include your child's potty preferences, such as reading books or singing songs, and provide the same rewards for them to give to your child for potty success. If you've been using a sticker chart at home, bring another to be used with the caregiver. If allowed, bring along the potty chair or insert your child is accustomed to using at home. You also want to make the caregiver aware of how you would like them to handle accidents: with no scolding and matter-of-fact reactions.

If possible, allow your caregiver to review your written plan in advance, so they can clarify any questions they may have. While they certainly have your child's best interests at heart, you don't necessarily want them thinking on the fly and doing something you don't agree with. See if the caregiver is willing to, at least loosely, keep track of the times your child uses the bathroom and/or has accidents, so you can continue observing your kiddo's potty schedule along with any differences between being with you versus being with them.

Open Communication

Before leaving your child in the care of someone else for the first time post–potty training, there are a couple of ways to ease your child into the transition. Open communication is going to be very important. Have a little conference between yourself, your child, and the caregiver where you both get down to eye level with your child and talk to them. To give a little ego boost, open the conversation with, "Can you tell Ms. Barbara how you've been using the potty like a big kid?" Then explain how their day will go. "She's going to help you use the potty today while Mommy is at work. If you feel like you need to go, you can just ask her. Right, Ms. Barbara?" Children love predictability, so you can even try a practice run with the caregiver while you're still there, so your child can see exactly how it will go and that there's nothing to worry about. It may also give them extra incentive to use the potty if they're able to call you throughout the day to report their potty success! (Of course, this has to workable for you and certainly isn't required.)

If your child goes to a daycare or caregiver instead of the caregiver coming to your home, before dropping them off, explore with your child the bathroom they'll be using. Really play up how cool and exciting it is. See if you can get them to say something they like about that bathroom (the paint color, the fuzzy rug, or a fancy shower curtain) to help them feel a connection and therefore feel more comfortable. See if they'll practice sitting on the potty while you're still there with them.

If they seem uneasy, show them how *you* can sit, or even offer for them to sit between your legs just so they can test it out.

As an optional extra motivator to use the potty correctly while you're away, you can promise a special surprise when you pick them up—maybe a new toy they've been wanting, or a stop at the ice cream shop on your way home. If the caregiver is able to remind them of the upcoming reward throughout the day, your child will be more likely to try harder in order to get their prize.

DEALING WITH DAYCARE

Potty training while your child attends a daycare center or preschool can have a lot of benefits, as well as pose some challenges. Actual institutions, whether public or private, may have more stringent policies regarding potty training than you would otherwise find at an in-home daycare, for example. These policies often stem from state regulations, so while it may be frustrating from a parent's perspective, in order for them to remain compliant as a facility, they need to adhere to them without much flexibility. That being said, similar to your preparations with other caregivers, you should always talk to the center's administrators about their potty training rules and practices *before* you start potty training at home. If your child spends a significant amount of time at daycare, then it may even make more sense to adapt any potty training you do with your child at home to the way it's done in their classroom, as opposed to the other way around.

There are plenty of awesome benefits to potty training while your child attends a daycare center. And depending on when you decide to start, it can actually pave the way for success at home, as well.

- **Peer pressure (in a good way!).** If your child sees their friends using the potty, they're more inclined to try it, too.

- **Set schedules.** Most classrooms will have set potty times when each child will sit on the potty, whether or not they need to go. This gives a lot of opportunities to practice and get comfortable with sitting on the toilet.

- **Learning the whole shebang.** In the classroom, teachers will show your child not only how to use the potty, but also how to pull pants up and down, and how to wash hands. It instills good potty practices from the get-go.

- **Experienced teachers.** Your child's teachers at daycare have worked on potty training with several (maybe hundreds of) kids of all different personalities and abilities. So they are well-equipped to handle even difficult potty learners.

- **Setting the stage.** Using the potty in the classroom helps potty training become part of your child's daily life, part of their routine. That way when it comes time to fully ditch the diapers, it won't seem like as big of a change to them.

- **Noting progress.** In many classrooms, potty progress is charted and documented. This is great information to have once you start potty training at home.

There are also some issues that may prove to be a little more challenging, but they don't need to be if you take them into account before starting potty training.

- **Not being able to use a small potty chair.** Most daycare centers don't allow the use of small floor potties (or even potty inserts) because of hygiene issues. That could potentially pose a challenge if your child is partial to their potty. Often, however, the toilets in daycare classrooms are "child size," which is actually a great way to transition your child from potty to toilet.

- **Not being able to use rewards.** There may be cases where your child's teachers aren't able to issue the same rewards you've been using at home, especially if it's a food item, because of choking and/or allergy issues. Not to mention, the teachers probably don't want to deal with a riot on their hands from giving a special treat to your child but not to anyone else!

- **A lot of children, not a lot of eyes.** Unfortunately, teachers in daycare centers are responsible for keeping an eye on many children at once, so they're always going in different directions. This makes it challenging for them to be able to watch your child closely enough to catch every one of their cues and signals, especially if they tend to be subtle.

- **Inability to support early potty learning.** Most daycare classrooms are set up to accommodate kids based on age group, with only a little flexibility when it comes to skill level. If your child is working on potty training at 18 months, they might still be too young in other areas to move up to the classroom where they're actively working on potty training. Take that into account when you're thinking of starting potty training.

- **Rotating staff.** This varies, but occasionally, your child will be interacting with multiple teachers throughout their day or week. Different teachers may have different approaches or practices when it comes to potty training. This could potentially make your child feel uneasy, depending on their personality. It also increases the risk of miscommunication, and staff could put your child in a disposable trainer unknowingly. If you don't want your child in disposable trainers or diapers anymore, make sure you remove all you'd provided to the school after you've communicated your wishes to the teachers.

- **Disposable trainers until fully trained.** Some centers are strict about keeping children in disposable trainers until they're considered "fully trained," which usually means that they are no longer having accidents, are dry through naps, and are either self-initiating or using the potty consistently at set times. You may find that you need to keep your child in disposable trainers while they're in school even when you have them diaper free at home. Since your child may be confused by the reintroduction of disposable trainers for school, the best solution is to inquire about the use of cloth diapers or cloth training pants instead. If that isn't allowed, see if you can have your child wear underwear underneath their disposable trainer so they're still aware of accidents. Otherwise, explain to your child that the disposable trainers are "special underwear" just for school.

Always request a parent-teacher conference to discuss potty training with the teacher who is most hands-on with your child throughout the day. Bring a copy of your progress chart (page 100) and any other relevant notes along with you for the meeting so you can review it all together and be on the same page to provide your child with the most consistent potty training experience possible.

SCRIPT

Are you looking for some helpful things to say to keep your child on track with potty training when out and about or in someone else's care? Use any or all of the following ideas and adapt them to work best for your child.

While out and about: "If you need to go potty, it's right over there. Just tell me and I will take you." (Physically point to the bathrooms.)

"We're going to be in the car for a little while, but we have your potty in the back. So just let me know if you need to go, and I can stop."

"Check out this cool bathroom! I really like that green rug! What do you like?"

Regarding disposable trainers for school: "These are your special school undies. Do your best to keep them dry all day, and if you do, I'll bring you a special treat when I pick you up!"

"It's back to school today! Remember to ask your teacher if you need help going potty."

CONSISTENCY IS KEY

As you're progressing through your potty training journey, especially with such a busy schedule, it can be easy to start neglecting the practice of praise and rewards you were giving your child in the very beginning. But until your child is consistently using the potty with no accidents, self-initiating most of the time (just taking themselves to the bathroom when they need to go), and staying dry through naps and overnight, there should still be an active level of training going on. So continue to be consistent with everything you've been doing so far. The longer you continue the positive reinforcement and rewards, the less likely there will be a regression. The amount of time this takes is going to vary from child to child because everyone's experience will be so different, but typically you can phase potty training into normalcy (meaning no more special treatment required) within about six to eight weeks.

Regular Routine

If you're working during the day while your child is in someone else's care, you can still create a routine and schedule for the times you are with your child: mornings, evenings, and weekends. As part of a busy family, it probably feels like you don't have even one spare second in the day, so having a set daily schedule or agenda can really help with your commitment to and consistency with potty training. Figuring out the best ways to make these changes can seem stressful. But it really doesn't have to feel overwhelming, and here's why: Number one, your child is learning a new skill that's ultimately going to make them more confident and independent, requiring less of your time and money by being done with diapers, *and* you get to help them do it. How cool is that!

Number two, you would most likely be changing diapers anyway, so just replace the diaper changing time with potty time!

Setting Habits

Even if you choose to keep your child in diapers overnight in the beginning, try to create a habit of sitting your child on the potty first thing when they wake up in the morning. Not only is this the most likely time to get pee in the potty (we all need to pee when we wake up in the morning!), but it also sets the stage for nighttime potty training. If you find that your child doesn't pee on the potty much or at all first thing in the morning, this probably means they already went in their diaper. In that case, wake them up 10 to 15 minutes or so before they would normally wake up, take off the diaper, and sit them on the potty right away. They should get a fair amount of pee in the potty at this point. And one less pee in the diaper is one step closer to being dry overnight. Now that's what I call progress!

From here, give your child some naked time or put them in underwear. If you need to send your child to daycare or their caregiver in cloth or disposable training pants, wait until you're heading out the door to put them on so your child doesn't get *too* comfortable with it, and so your explanation remains consistent and rings true that these are "school undies" only.

When you pick your child up at the end of the day, head home and change them back into regular underwear as soon as you can. In between wardrobe changes would be a good time to sit on the potty, unless they happened to go right before leaving school. While your child sits, you could have your daily recap conversation: "How was your day?" Factoring in potty time now could give you enough time to be able to read the mail or start dinner without being interrupted by potty breaks later. I would again recommend using the potty before bath time and last thing before getting into bed at night (and of course anytime in between if needed). These last two potty trips might seem too close together, but there's a method behind this madness, and it's called a "double void." Having your child go potty once at the beginning of their bedtime routine and then again right before they go to sleep helps ensure that your child's bladder is as empty as possible before going to bed, which helps promote nighttime dryness. I'll be covering even more about naptime and nighttime training in the next step.

Routine Changes

You see, potty training doesn't need to require a bunch of *additions* to your busy life, rather just some *changes* to your daily routine. There will probably be a slight learning curve in the beginning, but as the awesome parent you are, you'll quickly adapt and learn what works best for your family and lifestyle. Remember all that mental preparation you did in the beginning? Be sure you're carrying that same confidence and positivity all throughout the training process. This will really help you get through any challenging times. Believe me when I say that soon diapers and potty training will all be a distant memory, even though it might not seem like it right now. And don't forget to reward yourself with something you enjoy in the evenings, too—you deserve it!

TROUBLESHOOTING TECHNIQUES

My child never wants to use the bathroom when we're out in public.

This is very common. It takes most kids a long time to warm up to the idea of using the potty somewhere other than home. If they don't want to sit on the potty when you're out and about, don't push it. You have to have a certain level of trust. As long as they aren't having accidents, it is perfectly okay for them to hold it until they get home or to a place where they feel comfortable, which is why keeping their potty in the car or keeping an easy-to-carry insert on hand can be helpful and convenient.

Teachers report that my child is having accidents at school, even though they are doing so well at home.

Talk to the teacher and find out if the accidents tend to be around the same times each day. If this is the case—like daily during recess, for example—the teacher may need to prompt more often or change the timing of the prompts for your individual child.

My child wants to go potty everywhere. What can I do?

If you have an overly enthusiastic child who wants to go potty everywhere—restaurants, stores, museums—indulge their requests in the beginning so as not to discourage potty use. I promise that their heightened interest won't last forever!

No matter how much I try, my child's teacher and I cannot get on the same page.

Don't be afraid to get the daycare center's director or manager involved. In most cases, as long as you aren't requesting anything too extreme or something that's against their written policy, they will work with you. You pay them a lot of money, after all! Sometimes teachers can feel too overwhelmed to keep track of specific instructions for each child. The director can offer additional support and resources to ensure your child is getting the proper care.

We have so many activities going on after work/school that no two days are ever the same.

I completely understand how busy life can be between balancing multiple responsibilities—especially if you have multiple children in different sports or clubs, shared custody, medical treatments, PTA meetings, shift work, and the like. But even though it may seem chaotic and inconsistent to an outsider, that actually *is* consistency for your child if that's what they're already used to. There are certain elements of potty use that can carry over from day to day to reinforce the training, such as using the potty first thing in the morning and last thing before bed. Remember to stay confident! Your child will likely surprise you by showing how capable they are.

STEP 4 RECAP: FIVE TAKEAWAYS

1. Don't be afraid to take your potty training show on the road! Make up a "potty training survival kit" that you can easily grab on your way out the door. Your child will benefit from gaining experience using different potties in different places!

2. Always talk to caregivers and daycare providers *before* you begin potty training to find out their rules and policies, and then take those into account when organizing your own potty training plans.

3. Once you've introduced potty training at home and are ready to pass the baton to your caregiver and/or daycare, organize a conference with them to review your notes and progress chart (page 100) so everyone is on the same page.

4. Take some precautionary steps to help your child feel more comfortable using the potty in places other than home. Point out and explore bathrooms together in new places, meet with caregivers one-on-one so they can help your child feel more comfortable when they need help, and offer incentives for staying clean and dry throughout the day.

5. Consistency is key. Even in busy day-to-day life, do your best to create a potty routine for mornings, evenings, overnight, and weekends to keep advancing the learning process and to keep the expectations clear for your child

STEP 5
The Final Stretch

GUESS WHAT? YOU'RE ALMOST DONE! This step is going to cover the last few things you need to know to get your child down the home stretch. Mastering naptime, nighttime, and poop can prove to be some of the most challenging aspects of potty training. But continuing with the common theme of this book, if you're well-informed and know the approach you want to take before you get started, there's no need to worry! I am going to cover my best practices for each stretch of day and night so you can finally get to that coveted status of "fully potty trained."

NAPTIME

There are two main aspects to potty training during sleep. Number one is developing a brain-to-bladder connection, and number two is increasing muscle control. But the simple fact is most kids are ready for naptime (and nighttime) training well before their parents realize! Often, children will be dry during sleep and will pee in their diaper as soon as they wake up, giving the false impression that they've been peeing while asleep.

The natural progression to staying dry during sleep is as follows:

1. Peeing without being disrupted from sleep.

2. Peeing during sleep but waking up immediately afterward from the accident

3. Starting to pee while asleep and waking up in the middle of the accident.

4. Waking up before needing to pee.

5. Sleeping all the way through without needing to pee.

Keeping these steps in mind, you can begin to look for progress. So even if your child isn't staying dry the entire time they're asleep, you can find some level of accomplishment and know that things are moving in the right direction. If you're lucky, your child may skip some or all of these steps and go straight to being dry before potty training even starts!

Even if you aren't ready to ditch the diapers overnight just yet, the best way to test the waters with going diaper free while your child is asleep is to start with naptime.

Common Problems

Potty training for naptime can pose various challenges.

- **A lack of consistency in environment.** For example, your child may nap some days at preschool, once a week at a grandparent's house, and on weekends at home. This can make it harder to maintain a consistent process. Keep all caregivers on the same page as much as possible to avoid confusion for your child.

- **Daycare requirements.** Even if your child is already in underwear, most daycares automatically put children who aren't considered fully potty trained in a disposable trainer for naps. To maintain consistency, you want to be sure to communicate to your child's caregivers what your wishes are for naptime. If they require a disposable trainer for napping until your child shows they can be dry consistently, you may want to consider using a cloth diaper and a waterproof mattress cover for their cot instead.

- **Not limiting fluids.** By not limiting what your child is drinking before naptime, there is a greater chance of needing to pee while they're sleeping. But that's okay! It's better for your child to get in more liquids earlier in the day so you can limit them closer to bedtime for more dry nights. It's more likely they'll be able to hold their bladder for a two-hour nap than for 10 hours overnight anyway.

- **Still sleeping in a crib.** If your child still naps in a crib, they won't be able to get out of bed on their own if they have the urge to use the potty. Make sure you have a baby monitor in your child's room so they can call for you if they need to go.

- **The dreaded car nap.** If your child still isn't staying dry during naps, the last thing you want is them falling asleep in their car seat unprotected! But instead of using a disposable trainer, keep a waterproof car seat protector in your vehicle or potty training survival kit. Don't hesitate to use it to prevent a mess if there's any possibility your little one could fall asleep.

Best Strategies

For the fastest, most effective results, I recommend ditching naptime diapers at the same time as you initiate potty training. Not only does this keep things as consistent as possible for your child, but it also prevents them from potentially just withholding until they get their naptime disposable trainer on. Also, you are staying true to your word that there are no more diapers. Here are some of my best strategies to tackle potty training during naptime.

First and foremost, you want to be sure your child's mattress is protected in case of an accident. It can be very difficult to get urine stains and odor out of mattresses, and no one has time to deal with that! Next, on the days you're at home together, allow your child to nap bottomless for at least the first five naps. Even though your child is asleep, going bottomless still allows them to be more aware of their body's sensations and any accidents. A disposable trainer or underwear will just absorb the accident and not allow them to feel it, therefore never giving them the opportunity to experience Steps 2 and 3 of the natural progression mentioned on page 78. Encourage your child to sit on the potty to pee and/or poop before lying down for their nap. You can incorporate this as part of their regular routine so they will come to expect it. In addition, wake them up about 10 minutes before they normally would wake and have them sit on the potty at that time in order to prevent wetting the bed. If your child normally sleeps for two hours, wake them up at the one-hour 50-minute mark instead. If your child stays dry for their entire nap, be sure to offer a reward and lots of praise. You want them to feel proud and empowered!

Also, provide any specific information or instructions regarding naptime potty training to your child's caregivers so they are following the same process, setting your child up for success outside the home environment, as well.

Rest assured that as your child's daytime control improves and their potty frequency gradually decreases, they'll start having dry naps, too.

NIGHTTIME

The topic of nighttime potty training has proven to be somewhat controversial. Many people believe that being able to stay dry throughout the night is purely a result of hormonal development. It's true that there is a hormone called anti-diuretic hormone, or ADH, which we all produce as we get older, and it causes our bodies to make less urine overnight. This develops at different ages for everyone, and obviously this aspect cannot be taught or trained. But relying on this hormonal development alone has some risks. It can end up leaving you dependent on nighttime diapers for way longer than you intended (until your child is seven years of age or older), it can prolong daytime accidents, and by not training them to be dry overnight, the muscles your child uses to control their bladder may not fully strengthen. Although we can't teach our child how to *not* pee during the night, we can teach them how to wake up and get to the potty if they do need to pee. And *voilà*! Dry nights!

In order for your child to wake up from a deep sleep in the night to go to the potty, their brain needs to receive a signal from their bladder that it's full. With lots of patience and practice, you can help your kid learn to recognize this signal. Eventually your child will be able to go the entire night without needing to pee at all. As you start seeing bigger strides with their daytime potty training progress, you'll also start noticing overnight improvement. The earlier in the potty training process you decide to tackle nighttime training, the better. It may feel daunting in the beginning, but I'm going to give you the tools you need, so you have the confidence to get the job done!

Common Problems

As you can probably imagine, achieving dry nights can come with some challenges. They might include:

- **Lack of sleep.** You're probably worried about the lack of sleep that may come along with nighttime potty training. I won't lie to you—you might feel like you have a newborn again in the beginning, but I promise it's very temporary and very worth it!

- **Mountains of laundry.** I would recommend having multiple sheets and mattress pads on hand to avoid having to do laundry every single day. To keep middle-of-the-night bedclothes changes quick and easy, layer waterproof mattress pads and sheets so when the top layer gets wet, you can peel it away and have a clean, dry layer underneath. There are even some layered disposable sheets on the market that can just be thrown out if they get soiled.

- **Your child is a very deep sleeper.** It can definitely make things more challenging if your child is such a deep sleeper that they don't wake up from being wet. If your child is at least three years old, you can try a bedwetting alarm, which will wake your child at the first signs of wetness and thereby help create a brain-to-bladder connection.

Best Strategies

Overall, training for daytime and nighttime simultaneously is the best and most efficient way to see results. You could potentially do both together instead of having to take the time to go back and do nighttime training separately after you have a good handle on daytime training. Alternatively, if you're already balancing your child being in underwear at home and training pants at daycare anyway, you could opt for a more gradual approach and wait until your child is self-initiating and able to stay dry for longer periods throughout the day before starting nighttime potty training. Weigh the pros and cons as they relate to your family to decide on the best time to start.

For about a week before you begin, try doing "morning diaper checks," which I briefly mentioned in step 4. This can potentially save you some trouble (and sleep) in the long run. Here's how it works: About 15 minutes before your child normally wakes up in the morning, quietly go in and feel how wet their diaper is. This will tell you if they're peeing during the night or if they're waiting until they first wake up in the morning to release, which is actually very common. Make note of the results because you can use this information later.

As you did with naptime, you want your child to stay bottomless for at least the first five nights. Just like during daytime training, this aids in body awareness and the realization that there's no longer something there to catch the mess. In sleep, it will be difficult for your child to distinguish between underwear and a diaper.

It's also helpful to limit fluids after dinnertime. If your child usually takes milk or water in order to fall asleep, I'm not suggesting you take that away completely. Instead, cut the amount they normally get in half so it's no more than four ounces. The comfort they get is more about the habit of drinking than about the quantity. You should encourage your child to drink most of their fluids earlier in the day, so they still remain hydrated.

To facilitate your child's dryness, incorporate the double void I mentioned in the previous step into your nightly routine. Again, this just means have your child pee once at the beginning of their bedtime routine and then again right before they climb into bed.

Since your child has never experienced a night without diapers, there are some steps you can take to make them feel more at ease about the change. First, keep their small potty beside their bed, or make sure they have a clear, short path to the bathroom. Let them know it's okay to get out of bed and use the potty if they need to or to call you for help. Make sure their room is dimly lit—enough to see where they're going, but not so bright that they fully wake up. You can even do a practice run so they understand how it will go, which can be fun, yet practical.

Remember the diaper checks I mentioned? Here's where they come into play. If your child's diapers mostly felt dry (or even just slightly wet), you can skip over this part of the training—hooray! If not, get your child out of bed 10 minutes before they normally wake up and have them sit on the potty. Start your day off with one potty success already in the bag!

On the other hand, if they still felt pretty wet during diaper checks, to facilitate dryness, you can try up to two "dream pees" each night. A dream pee involves you lifting your child out of bed and onto their potty to relieve themselves and then putting them back into bed without fully waking them. The first can be done around 10 or 11 p.m. before you go to sleep yourself, to prevent *you* from having to wake up twice (you're welcome!). The second is usually effective around 3 or 4 a.m. From there, your child should be able to stay dry until morning. If your child really protests the dream pees or doesn't go back to sleep afterward easily, feel free to discontinue them. You'll still see results—you just may have to change the sheets a few extra times. If your child is already wet when you attempt the dream pee, adjust the timing a bit the next night until you find the right balance. Gradually, you can move the times forward or back by an hour every couple of days until they are eliminated altogether.

If your child ever wakes from an accident, the best thing to do is have them sit on the potty while you change their bedclothes. They most likely didn't fully void their bladder in the bed, so you can potentially get a little success out of it!

SCRIPT

From whispered messages to frank potty talk, the following lines will plant positive seeds that will grow overnight.

"Don't go potty in your bed."
By whispering this each night right before your child goes to sleep, it stays with them.

"Remember your potty is right here next to your bed if you feel like you need to go."

"Let's try to hear one more drop."
This can be helpful if your child doesn't feel like they need to go just before bedtime.

"Food goes in, our body uses up the good stuff, then poop comes out. It's kind of like trash. That's why we put it in the potty. We wouldn't carry around an old granola bar wrapper all day, would we? Yucky!"
Talk to your child about how the body works so they don't feel possessive of their poop.

POOP

You know the old adage "Sh*t happens"? Well, unfortunately, it doesn't always happen easily during potty training. Poop training can take longer to master than pee training because there are fewer opportunities to practice. If you miss one, you may have to wait an entire day or more before you get the next. If you notice your child struggling with pooping on the potty once they've gone diaper free, it's important that you address this quickly before it gets too far out of control. I'm going to give you some of my best tips and tricks to handle any challenges that could arise!

Common Problems

Getting your child to poop on the potty can be, well, crappy. In fact, in a group of parents that I surveyed, more than 70 percent said getting their child to poop on the potty was the one thing they struggled with the most. So if this happens to you, know you aren't alone! Some common issues with pooping can include:

- **A genuine fear.** Some children have a real fear of pooping on the potty. It's hard for us adults to comprehend, but to them, that fear is very real. It could be the sounds, the sensations (it can feel as if part of their body is falling out—scary, right?), the splash from the toilet, a painful bowel movement in the past, or something else. The first step is to embrace your child's fear, and validate it for them without making it worse. If your child feels understood, they'll feel more at ease and more willing to listen to you. Next, you need to have *a lot* of patience and to provide *a lot* of encouragement. Try to find what brings them comfort, and be there for your child to help them over the hump. Usually after a couple of poops in the potty, the fear fades away.

- **Withholding poop.** Before you assume your child is withholding poop, remember that poop frequency tends to naturally decrease once potty training starts. So a once-a-day pooper may go to every other day, and so on. If your child hasn't pooped for three days or more and is obviously uncomfortable, you want to take action so their bowel movement is easy to pass once they do go. More about this below.

- **Insisting on a diaper to poop in.** Some kids will be completely fine with peeing on the potty and will wear underwear all day with no accidents, but when it comes time to poop, they'll request a diaper. This is usually a result of stubbornness or resistance to change. As hard as it is, try not to give in. If you do, you'll send your child a mixed message, and they'll never fully learn what is expected of them. The process will be prolonged even further.

- **Not knowing how to poop on the potty.** When a child is wearing a diaper, they can poop in a number of different positions: standing, squatting, or lying down. So when it comes time to poop on the toilet, they may not fully know how to poop in a seated position with their legs dangling. This is why a small floor potty is recommended so they are able to put their feet flat on the floor for support and to bear down. If your child typically squats while pooping, you can have them put their feet up on a step stool to mimic that position. It also helps to invite your child into the bathroom with you while you go, so you can talk them through how to push and how your stomach feels before versus after.

Best Strategies

A lot of "poop problems" stem from a bowel movement in the past that was uncomfortable or painful, whether we were aware of it or not. Your child may hold onto that memory and start to associate pooping with pain, especially if you take away the comfort of their diaper. To avoid this from becoming a problem for them again, be sure you're doing what it takes to keep their bowel movements soft, comfortable, and easy to pass. You can do this in various ways, such as giving a daily probiotic, offering a balanced diet high in healthy fats (foods like avocados, olive oil, coconut oil, full-fat yogurt, and nut butters) and fiber, and encouraging lots of water. Alternatively, you can opt for a gentle over-the-counter stool softener containing polyethylene glycol 3350, which is very effective in a pinch (be sure to check with your pediatrician for proper dosage).

As a general rule of thumb, the best time to catch a bowel movement is 20 to 30 minutes after lunch or dinner. Either you or their caregiver can have your child sit on the potty at those times for approximately 10 minutes. This, in combination with the diet/supplement changes mentioned above, can create a "poop schedule," making your child's poop routine regular and predictable.

If your child struggles with releasing poop while sitting on the potty, it could be because they feel a need for privacy. This is especially true if they would hide to poop when they were in diapers. Once you get your child set up on the potty with a distraction of some sort, walk away for a minute or two. This will ease any performance anxiety, and they'll likely go while you aren't in the room!

If privacy doesn't seem to be an issue, there are some other options to try. Physical activity is a great way to promote healthy bowels, especially running and jumping. If you suspect your child needs to poop but it isn't quite there yet, get active! Play a quick game of tag or do some jumping jacks, and that should help things along. Additionally, while they're sitting on the potty, allow them to blow bubbles or make a pinwheel spin. Not only does this help relax the bowel, but it activates the same muscles we use to push out poop. While your child is distracted and having fun, they could end up pooping without even realizing it!

Medical Issues

Sometimes, poop problems can progress into medical issues that require diagnosis and treatment from a professional. The most common condition that can develop is constipation, which usually results from withholding or dehydration. If the diet changes or the over-the-counter treatments mentioned above aren't showing results, you may need to reach out to your doctor.

In some cases, although rare, chronic constipation can develop into a more severe condition known as encopresis. This is when hard, dry stool builds up in the lower intestine as a result of prolonged constipation, weakening muscle structure and making regular bowel movements difficult or impossible to pass. Symptoms include frequent leakage of stool (very soft, almost diarrhea-like), often without your child realizing it, avoiding bowel movements, loss of appetite, and frequent pee accidents. This is usually diagnosed with abdominal imaging or X-rays, and requires a strict laxative regimen as treatment.

If you ever suspect a medical problem is holding your child back from potty success, it's important to seek proper treatment before revisiting potty training. Your little one's health should always come first!

TROUBLESHOOTING TECHNIQUES

My child's sleep accidents aren't improving. Is there anything else I can do?
If it's been several days and you aren't seeing much progress when it comes to nap or nighttime training, you're probably looking for a new strategy. Overnight accidents aren't your child's fault, and you should never punish or scold. But it can help your child "own" the accidents more if you get them involved in the cleanup process. Have them assist in changing the sheets and the laundry, not as a punishment, but as a consistent result of the behavior.

My child continually sleeps through their accidents.
If your child sleeps so deeply that they aren't disrupted by nighttime accidents, there are some measures you can take to help. Make bedtime a half hour earlier, or extend your "quiet time" before your child goes to sleep to avoid overtiredness. Adding an extra night-light in their room can also prevent excessive deep sleep. Bedwetting alarms can be very effective in these cases, as well.

My child still sleeps in a crib. How do I handle nighttime potty training?
Still being in a crib is not a deal-breaker when it comes to nighttime potty training. It can be a little more physically strenuous on you, because you'll have to lift your child out of the crib and onto

the potty for the dream pees if you opt to do them. Be sure you have a baby monitor to listen for your child calling for you. *Hint:* If you ever hear your child wake upset in the night, it could mean they either need to go potty or have had an accident. As hard as it can be, try to jump into action as soon as possible. If you planned on transitioning to a big kid bed anytime in the near future, you should do that and wait for the new sleeping arrangements to settle in *before* starting nighttime potty training.

My child poops in their nighttime diaper.

This can become a common problem, and unless you get rid of the nighttime diapers, it can be a hard habit to break. Your child is likely waiting until nighttime because of a combination of a desire for privacy and the comfort of their diaper. Use a calendar to count down the nights to no more nighttime diapers with your child, just like you did for daytime. When you take the diapers away, make sure you have their small potty available to them in their room, and don't be afraid to offer a reward to give them extra motivation to use it!

STEP 5 RECAP: FIVE TAKEAWAYS

1. In order for your child to be fully potty trained, you'll need to ditch the diapers for naps and overnight, as well. It's most efficient to do it all at the same time, but if you're looking for a more gradual approach, you can start with naps and move forward from there.

2. Make sure your child's caretakers and daycare staff are on the same page when it comes to naptime to maintain consistency and avoid any confusion for your child.

3. When you eliminate diapers for sleep, be sure you have a small potty next to your child's bed for easy access. A dimly lit room works best—enough light to see, but not to fully wake them.

4. One week before starting nighttime potty training, perform diaper checks about 10 minutes before your child normally wakes up in the morning to gauge how much they're peeing in the night. To facilitate nighttime training, make use of techniques such as limiting fluids, the double void, and dream pees.

5. While very common, poop problems such as withholding, not being able to release, or outright stubbornness can present themselves and should be addressed as soon as you notice them, to keep from creating bad habits.

A FINAL NOTE
Continue Teaching and Learning

CONGRATULATIONS! WELL DONE! You're well on your way to having yourself a fully potty trained kiddo, which means you're on your way to buying your last pack of diapers! Things may not be perfect just yet, but you should feel very proud of your child *and* yourself for how far you've already come! Please remember that everyone's potty training journey is different, so be mindful not to compare yours with anyone else's. The most important thing is that progress is being made, period.

BITTERSWEET SUCCESS

Speaking of progress, here are some examples of how yours might look so far. It could be one or any combination of these scenarios, depending on the approach you've taken. You're seeing many fewer daytime accidents (if any at all), meaning improved muscle control and greater body awareness. Your child is using the potty when prompted without resistance when in your care, as well as when they're with others. They may even be self-initiating and using public bathrooms occasionally by now. You're seeing at least a few poop successes, which is no easy feat! And if you've started potty training during sleep periods, your child is having some dry naps and nights here and there. I hope this helps put into perspective the fruits of your labor, all while balancing your already busy schedule!

Potty training can be one of the most challenging hurdles of childhood. At the same time, it's also one of the best ways to instill pride, confidence, and independence in your child. As a mom myself, I know it can be a little bittersweet to see your baby growing up, but the amount of pride they exude when mastering this new skill completely makes up for the "bitter" part.

Keep in mind that there's going to be a certain level of maintenance and upkeep you'll need to do to keep things moving in the right direction. But the good news is the basics have been instilled, which means the *really* hard work is done. Soon, you'll be struggling to remember what changing a diaper was like!

UNCOMMON ISSUES

Although uncommon, sometimes an event in your child's life can cause a disruption to their potty training progress, even if they were already fully potty trained. Unforeseen circumstances such as injury, illness, trauma (physical or emotional), or anything that results in a large amount of stress for your child can cause them to regress.

A potty training regression is when an otherwise potty trained child suddenly starts having multiple, reoccurring accidents. If this is happening with your child, step one is to try and figure out what may have caused the regression in the first place. That way, you can be better equipped to help them cope. Young children haven't always learned how to process emotion, so it's up to you to help them work through whatever they're feeling. Provide many opportunities to talk and keep the lines of communication open, but don't force them into talking if they don't want to. You always want to validate their feelings by using phrases like "I understand," and "It's okay to feel that way," and "I've felt that way, too." Try to help them look for something positive in the situation. For example, if their emotional stress stems from an injury, say, "I understand you're upset because you can't play soccer right now. But at least you can eat lots of ice cream until you get better!"

The best thing you can do is maintain consistency. Go along with your regular routine as much as possible. Remember, children find comfort in predictability. Do your best to ensure your child is eating healthfully and getting plenty of exercise. Both will help them sleep better and balance their moods and emotions. You may need to backtrack in the potty training process a bit as far as prompting at appropriate times or using rewards for success, but do not go back to diapers. For the most part, regressions will clear themselves up within a couple of weeks.

In more severe cases, it may be too much for you alone to help your child cope. If four weeks have gone by and accidents aren't improving, your child isn't able to function properly at school or at home, you notice any drastic changes in their behavior, or the stress has started resulting in physical discomfort (headaches or stomachaches, for example), it may be in your child's best interest to contact a counselor or mental health professional.

KEEP AT IT

There are many hidden benefits to potty training that are less obvious than ditching the diapers. You also developed new skills for interacting with and caring for your child that you can apply to other aspects of parenting, as well. Continue to utilize what you've learned as your child grows!

The potty training process gets you to think about your child in ways you may not have otherwise. You've probably learned a lot about them: their personality type, how they learn, what motivates them, and more. You'll likely find yourself reaching back into your pocket for those tools the next time your child is learning something new—the alphabet, how to write, how to tie their shoes, and lots more. And knowing, really knowing, your child on this level is only going to further increase the bond you share with them.

You've also learned how to help your child adapt to change. With potty training being one of the biggest changes your child has experienced in their little life so far, you probably got a good taste of how they respond and react to new things. Maybe it was a total breeze, and if it was, that's great! Or maybe it was a bit of a challenge, or worse. But if that was the case, you learned how to help them come to terms with something new. So now you can apply those same principles in the future if you experience their resistance toward change.

In addition to getting to know your child, you also learned how to effectively communicate with your child's caregivers and teachers. There may have been *a lot* of communication among different people to make this potty training thing a success. And the truth is, this is just the beginning! There are many years of interaction to come with your child's future babysitters, teachers, and coaches. The more involved you are in your child's supervision and education, the better care they will receive.

I also hope you've realized how beneficial it is to focus on the successes and, as hard as it may be sometimes, to maintain a positive attitude—not just in parenting, but in all aspects of life. Don't ever hesitate to take a minute to pat yourself on the back. Just as your child deserved praise in their potty training, you deserve it for all of your hard work, too!

PROGRESS CHART

How much liquid does your child drink before needing
to pee?

_____

How many times an hour does your child pee?

_____

How long can they hold their bladder?

_____

How often does your child poop, and at what time(s) of day?

_____

How does your child's behavior change when using the
potty? What are their cues?

_____

_____

_____

Does your child prefer privacy or for you to be in the room?

_____

What are your child's potty preferences? Do they like to read
a particular book or sing a special song?

_____

_____

What terminology do you use when prompting your child to use the potty or when talking about the potty?

_____

How do you handle successes? What rewards do you offer?

_____

_____

_____

How do you handle accidents?

_____

What is your child's naptime routine?

_____

Other notes:

_____

_____

_____

_____

_____

_____

_____

_____

RESOURCES

Here are some other helpful resources I've compiled to supplement your potty training experience.

Websites

HealthyChildren.org. "Toilet Training." https://www.healthychildren.org/English/ages-stages/toddler/toilet-training/Pages/default.aspx.

Kids Health. "Toilet Training." https://kidshealth.org/en/parents/toilet-teaching.html.

Autism Speaks. "Toilet Training Guide." https://www.autismspeaks.org/sites/default/files/2018-08/Toilet%20Training%20Guide.pdf.

American Academy of Pediatrics. "Toilet Training." https://www.aap.org/en-us/advocacy-and-policy/aap-health-initiatives/practicing-safety/Pages/Toilet-Training.aspx.

HealthyChildren.org. "Toilet Training Children with Special Needs." https://www.healthychildren.org/English/ages-stages/toddler/toilet-training/Pages/Toilet-Training-Children-with-Special-Needs.aspx.

Books for Grown-ups

Faber, Adele and Elaine Mazlish. **How to Talk So Kids Will Listen and Listen So Kids Will Talk.** New York: Scribner, 2012.

Jandu, Allison. **The Poop Puzzle: What To Do if Your Child Will Not Poop on the Potty.** Independently published, 2018.
If you've gone through potty training but your child's poop situation is not improving, this guide will help you determine *why* your child is experiencing the problem, and the best ways to handle it for your specific situation.

Spock, Benjamin. **The Common Sense Book of Baby and Child Care.** Mountain View, CA: Ishi Press, 2013.

Tobin, Cathryn. **The Parent's Problem Solver: Smart Solutions for Everyday Discipline Dilemmas and Behavioral Problems**. New York: Three Rivers Press, 2002.

Books for Kids

Here are some of my favorite potty training–related children's books that your little one is sure to love!

Hochman, David and Ruth Kennison. **The Potty Train**. New York: Simon & Schuster Books for Young Readers, 2008.

Markes, Julie. **Where's the Poop?** New York: HarperFestival, 2004.

Moyle, Eunice and Sabrina Moyle. **Super Pooper and Whizz Kid: Potty Power!** New York: Harry N. Abrams, 2018.

Pap, Mary. **The Potty Fairy**. Minneapolis: Mill City Press, Inc., 2018.

Van Genechten, Guido. **I've Got to Go**. Belgium: Clavis, 2017.

INDEX

ACKNOWLEDGMENTS

FIRST AND FOREMOST, I HAVE TO THANK MY BABIES,
Evan and Layla. Without you two, I would not be where I am
today. I would probably still be wandering—not lost, but not
found either. Thank you for teaching me a love I never would have
known and for giving me my place in this world. You are my life,
my reason. As you get older, I hope you are inspired by me even a
fraction of the amount that I am inspired by you every single day.

To my amazingly patient husband, Raj—the most selfless
person I've ever known—thank you for supporting me through the
late nights and long hours and never complaining for a second,
for keeping the kids out of my hair while I was working on this
project without me ever even having to ask, and for your effort-
less ability to provide for us, busting your butt at work so I can be
home with our babies and grow my own business as an author and
entrepreneur. You were as important to my completing this book
as I was. Thank you so much, babe.

I'm so thankful for my parents. Mom and Dad, you guys are
truly the best parents anyone could ask for. Without your love,
help, and unwavering belief in me, I wouldn't have half the cour-
age I needed to have taken on this book or anything else. I can only
hope Evan and Layla love me as much as I love both of you. Thank
you for all you have done and continue to do for us.

Thank you to Sarah and Nicole, my two very best friends, loudest cheerleaders, and the greatest aunties on the planet. You know we go way back, like *back* back—so much so that we don't even consider each other friends, but sisters. I mean, you both bought all of my potty training books even though you don't have kids. That's friendship at its finest. I love you both.

To Winnie and David, thank you for always making me blush with your praise, support, and compliments. You have a way of helping me realize and appreciate my accomplishments that I probably wouldn't otherwise, and I am so grateful to you for that. I wish we were closer together, but I love you guys so much.

Trying to organize all the potty training information within this cluttered mom-brain of mine into a book that people can read and understand was challenging, but not difficult, thanks to my amazing editor, Barbara. Thank you for reading my mind, keeping me straight, and understanding my humor. It was an absolute pleasure working with you.

Being asked to author a book is a surreal, yet validating, experience. Thank you to my publisher, Callisto Media, for recognizing my expertise even when my profession as a potty training consultant is laughed at by so many.

Thank you to all of my clients who have allowed me to go on their potty training journey with them, putting their faith in me during what can be a very sensitive and intimate time, and for unknowingly letting me learn from them. I hold a special place in my heart for each and every one of you.

Finally, thank you to my entire family for loving me and being proud of me. You have all played a part in my getting here, whether you know it or not.

ABOUT THE AUTHOR

ALLISON JANDU is a professional consultant who assists families with one of childhood's most important, yet daunting, milestones—potty training.

Allison has helped hundreds of children of all ages and abilities. Her custom potty training plans are based on building independence and empowerment, and she thrives on seeing children succeed. She has made it her personal mission to revolutionize the way we think about potty training as a society.

Allison is also a mother and holds a bachelor of science from the University of Baltimore. She has instructed childcare professionals and written internationally accredited continuing education training materials. In addition to *Potty Training in 5 Easy Steps*, she has written two highly praised potty training guides: *The Poop Puzzle* and *The Wee Hours*.